# the Abbey
# Cookbook

# A the ABBEY COOKBOOK

### Inspired Recipes from the Great Atlanta Restaurant

Hans Bertram

THE HARVARD COMMON PRESS
Harvard, Massachusetts

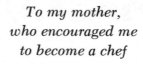

*To my mother,*
*who encouraged me*
*to become a chef*

*and to my wife*
*Heidi*

The Harvard Common Press
The Common, Harvard, Massachusetts 01451

Copyright 1982 by The Harvard Common Press, Inc.

Printed in the United States of America

**Library of Congress Cataloging in Publication Data**

Bertram, Hans.
    The Abbey cookbook.

    Includes index.
    1. Cookery, International.   2. Abbey Restaurant.
I. Title.
TX725.A1B473          641.59         81-20225
ISBN 0-916782-23-9                  AACR2
ISBN 0-916782-26-3 (spiral bdg.)

Special Editor: Leslie A. Hanna
Photographs by Larry Thomas
Cover design by Paul Bacon

10  9  8  7  6  5

# about
# the abbey

I N THE HEART of downtown Atlanta, minutes from the
ultramodern towers of the convention hotels that rise
above the city, there stands an old church. The soft red of
its bricks stands out against the bustling street corner of
Piedmont and Ponce de Leon; its bell tower rises in massive, ornate
dignity towards the sky. Outside, a small sign marks the awninged
entranceway. This is the Abbey, Atlanta's finest old-world dining
place.

Inside the Abbey, there is an atmosphere of hushed grandeur
that is brought about first of all by the magnificence of the interior.
Vaulted ceilings soar fifty feet overhead. Stained glass windows
glow their brilliant colors into the dusk. Heavy wooden tables and
high-backed monastery chairs are spaced throughout the nave, the
raised altar platform, the sanctuary. Waiters in the brown robes of
monks serve those who dine, moving swiftly and quietly at their
tasks. And in the choir loft a harpist plays, bathed in a pool of light,
angelic.

The mood of reverence that is stirred by the surroundings at the Abbey is only enlarged and completed by the food that is served at the candlelit tables. The cuisine at the Abbey is breathtaking. More than one hundred choices of soups, appetizers, salads, vegetables, main courses, and desserts are offered; and each is prepared with as much loving attention to detail as if it were being served to an honored guest in the chef's own dining room. The style is continental, eclectic, classical with a dash of nouvelle cuisine; each dish, however minor, is presented with a decorative flair that transforms it into art. It is clear that there is a person behind this food who cares passionately that it approach perfection. Hans Bertram's kitchen at the Abbey is, in truth, inspired.

It is because of Hans himself, of course, that the menu at the Abbey as well as the preparation of the food shows such a wide range of excellence. Hans Bertram grew up in Braunschweig, West Germany, and went through a classical European training in all areas of a hotel kitchen. He had always cherished a desire to travel, and on the completion of his training he signed on as a saucier on the Dutch ocean liner "New Amsterdam." After absorbing the Dutch and Indonesian influences of such a position, he was able to move on to the Scandinavian kitchen of a first-class hotel in Stockholm. Another chef saucier position prompted his return to Germany; and then, in 1964, he accepted the first of a series of growing responsibilities in large hotel kitchens in South Africa. It is clear that by the time Hans Bertram came to the United States in 1967, his culinary style had developed and expanded to include the best of a variety of world cuisines.

The cooking style of the American South only enhanced this background. As Hans Bertram advanced in his career, working for major hotel and restaurant kitchens throughout the South, his recipes picked up an occasional regional accent that broadened his culinary base still further. By the time he took over the Abbey restaurant kitchen in 1973, his talents were at their peak; and the spectacular success the Abbey has enjoyed over the years since then—the prestigious Travel/Holiday Award for seven consecutive years, and others too numerous to mention—bespeaks this better than anything else.

Owner Bill Swearingen moved the Abbey from its original, small location in another Atlanta church in 1977. Its new home, which had been built in 1915 to house a Methodist Episcopalian congregation in Atlanta's most fashionable neighborhood, almost doubled the seating capacity of the restaurant; and Swearingen installed the most modern computer facilities to insure that orders were handled promptly and efficiently.

The efficiency of the kitchen at the Abbey is indeed one of its most remarkable aspects. To maintain consistently superb quality in the cuisine while serving as many as four hundred patrons in an evening requires the utmost in organization—and all one need do is step inside the Abbey kitchen to realize that this is a kingdom of its own. Spotless counters stretch across the red tiled floor, and gleaming copper pots and pans hang easily accessible to the chefs. Sauces are newly prepared daily from huge stock pots that simmer in the back kitchen; at the height of the dinner hour they stand ready to receive the final touches before they accompany a freshly prepared entree. Assistant chefs work swiftly at their stations, with no appearance of rush. Plates are garnished and given the final touches until their appearance is perfect. Waiters in their brown robes line up to pick up the dishes within seconds of their completion, and Hans Bertram stands by to check every plate before it goes to the table. And in the midst of it, night chef Reginald Moss tears the orders from the computer printer and calls them out in his ringing voice now to the chefs, now to the waiters, keeping the rhythm of the great kitchen moving ahead until the last plate has been carried upstairs to where the celebration of dinner continues to the hushed clink of silver and glasses, the murmur of conversation.

Reginald is but one example of the professional staff that has made the Abbey what it is. Like many of the chefs at the restaurant, Reginald trained under Hans Bertram; in fact, he started at the Abbey as a dishwasher when he was only fourteen years old. In addition, there is Charlie Howard, who has worked as head chef under Hans for several years; and there are the brothers Bennie and Darius Gilmere—known as "Smokey" and "Sly"—who serve as saucier and entremetier, and who have worked with Hans for close to a decade, coming to the Abbey from posts as chefs in smaller operations. Finally, two great European culinary artists add their distinction to the Abbey kitchen: Guy Mougel, whose experience as a pastry chef in his native France has made him the creator of many prizewinning confections since his arrival in America in 1959; and Swiss butcher Emil Stussi, whose skill with every aspect of cutting and preparing fine meats has made the Abbey's reputation for the best viands in the city.

Dining room operations are carried out under the command of George Gore, the Abbey's imposing manager and wine expert. George supervises the staff of waiters, ensures that every table is attended to with style and grace, and recommends wine from the Abbey's extensive cellar. Like many gourmet diners, George prefers California wines for their fine, subtle qualities and their reasonable prices; and he has contributed his suggestions throughout this book for two wines that might accompany each entree that is described.

All the dishes that are presented here are specialties at the Abbey; they have been requested time and again over the years by those who have enjoyed them. Where there is a "chef's secret," it has been gladly given; no special ingredients or procedures have been omitted. Though they originated in Hans Bertram's restaurant kitchen, the recipes have been carefully scaled down for the home chef and tested again in the Abbey kitchen to ensure their accuracy. Aside from a modest assortment of pots and pans, a few good knives, and perhaps a food processor or blender, there is little special equipment needed to prepare the same food one might have marveled at in the Abbey's dining room. What is necessary is the freshest food one can acquire—a cardinal rule at the Abbey, where everything is prepared fresh daily—and the willingness to pay careful attention to every aspect of its preparation. Then, one will succeed in presenting true "Abbey food" to one's guests—and enjoy the reputation for excellence that these recipes have for years inspired.

—The Harvard Common Press
January 1982

# Contents

*Eight pages of color photographs
appear between pages 84 and 85.
Captions are on page 84.*

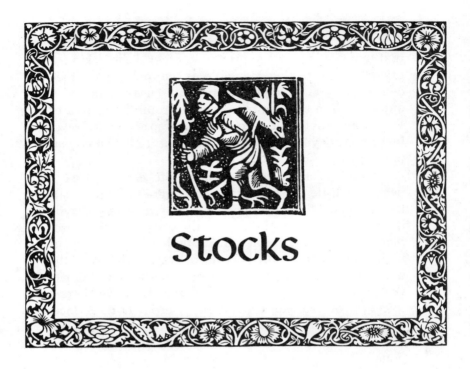

# Stocks

HE MOST ESSENTIAL INGREDIENT to all my cooking at the Abbey—and, in fact, to the cooking of any fine chef—is the stock that I prepare at the outset. Whether it is made from beef, veal, chicken, or fish, whether it is a clear stock or a brown stock, it will serve as the basis for dozens of the recipes I present in this collection. Its secrets are what lie behind the special flavor of a cream sauce or a wine sauce, or the elusive "something" that makes a gourmet's soup taste different from the rest. It is delightfully ironic that to make a fine stock only the simplest ingredients are required: bones and scraps, common kitchen vegetables and spices, cold water—and plenty of time.

Procure uncooked bones and scraps from your butcher or fish market when you plan to make any stock. Even good cooks often mistakenly use the leftover bones from a dinner they have enjoyed; and although these can contribute to a good soup, the essence of their flavor has already been considerably depleted. The stock must embody that essence, and requires fresh, uncooked ingredients—though they can be parts of the meat, fowl, or fish that one would avoid in preparing other dishes: skin, heads, organs are perfectly acceptable as the makings of stock. Of course, if your recipe involves the use of boiled meat anyway—in a chicken fricassee, for example, or in a cream sauce that calls for diced cooked veal—go ahead and save time by preparing your stock from the meat itself, which you can use later.

Onion, celery, carrots, the white ends of leeks, and perhaps a little parsley are the only ingredients necessary for the "mirepoix," the chopped vegetable mixture that will join the cooking bones and scraps in the stockpot. These are supplemented by the simple but subtle basic spices and herbs, which should be fresh whenever possible: bay leaves, thyme, basil, salt, black pepper, and sometimes a hint of clove in a veal or chicken stock. Remember that whatever herbs and spices flavor your stock should not overpower its essence; the basic stock must be adaptable to its different uses later in sauces and soups, which may then carry widely varying additional flavorings of their own. Wine, for example, while it has its place in a brown stock or a fish stock, is not an ingredient I recommend for the other clear stocks; let the wine be added later, to fit the particular dish you are preparing.

Except for a brown stock, which resembles a sauce almost more than a stock, the basic procedure for preparing a stock will not vary. In the bottom third of a gallon pot the cook will put the bones, scraps, mirepoix vegetables, and herbs and spices; the pot will then be filled perhaps three quarters full with cold water, and brought to a boil. It is crucial that cold water be used at the start; this opens the pores of the bones and allows their flavor to escape more completely while the water is heating. After the boil, the mixture whould simmer for several hours without a cover; this reduces the amount of liquid, but also contributes to a clear rather than a cloudy stock. The final step is to strain the stock, which will yield about half a gallon of liquid. The stock is then ready to use, or to freeze in pint-sized containers for later.

Brown stock in its many incarnations—including the more concentrated demi-glace and glace de viande—is started, on the other hand, by roasting bones and mirepoix, with perhaps some bits of leftover bacon, in fat in the oven to impart a rich, dark flavor. Tomato paste joins the mixture and is braised, adding a rosy hue; and sometimes flour is added for thickening at this point. Finally the water—or in some cases, a beef stock—is added, and the brew is then simmered and strained just like a clear stock. Dark brown and shiny, the brown stock makes the basis for innumerable wine sauces and brown sauces, thick soups and stews.

Almost all stocks will keep in the refrigerator eight to ten days without spoiling—except for fish, which is more temperamental and will probably not last for more than four or five days. Any stock, though, can be frozen for several months with good results.

Whatever the stock, however, its most reduced form will always be a great help to the gourmet chef. The various reductions you prepare—glace de viande, glace de poisson, glace de volaille—can be kept refrigerated or put in the freezer and easily reconstituted by adding water when you need them. (If you freeze them in very small quantities, perhaps in an ice tray, they will be ready for immediate use in flavoring a sauce or soup. The rich, essential flavors of the reductions you prepare are probably the most important ingredients in all the cooking you will do; so it is well worth your while to have them always on hand.

# Fonds de Boeuf
## Beef Stock
*Yields 3 quarts*

*This stock can be made either with beef bones only or with a combination of bones and meat, according to your preference.*

> 3 onions, unpeeled
> 6-7 pounds beef bones *or* 3 pounds beef bones *plus* 1½ pounds beef and trimmings (shank meat, brisket, or lean ground beef)
> 2 carrots
> 2 stalks celery
> 2 leeks (white ends only)
> 1 clove garlic, peeled
> ½ bunch parsley
> Thyme, several fresh sprigs or ½ teaspoon dried
> Basil, two fresh sprigs or ¼ teaspoon dried
> 5-6 bay leaves
> 10-15 black peppercorns
> 1½ teaspoons salt

Wash unpeeled onions and cut in half. Sear the cut surface of the onion halves until blackened. Do this directly on a burner or in an ungreased skillet. (This assures your stock the right golden brown color.) Wash other vegetables and chop into large pieces.

Lay bones (and/or meat), and vegetables in a soup pot. Pour one gallon cold water over these and bring to a boil. Skim off any scum that may rise to the surface now and later during simmering. Reduce heat and add garlic, herbs, salt, and pepper. Simmer, uncovered, for three to four hours. Correct seasonings if necessary.

Strain through a fine sieve or cheesecloth. Reserve only the broth. (Remove any meat from bones for use later in soup or another dish.)

Degrease now or after refrigerating until the fat solidifies on the surface.

## fonòs Brun
## Brown Stock
*Yields 3 to 4½ quarts*

*Veal bones, pork bones, and a small proportion of beef bones may combine in this very useful stock. I recommend using bones from the loin, rib, shank, and knuckle. With the brown stock, one may go on to make the essential glace de viande and demi-glace, given as variations here.*

> 4-6 quarts beef and/or veal stock (page 7)
> ¼ cup vegetable oil
> 7 pounds chopped veal and/or pork bones (small pro-portion of beef bones is optional)
> 2 carrots
> 2 stalks celery
> 2 leeks, white ends only
> 2 onions, unpeeled
> Leftover tomato ends and mushroom stems, optional
> 2 cloves garlic, unpeeled
> 1 small bunch parsley
> Thyme, 1 sprig fresh or ¼ teaspoon dried
> 5-6 bay leaves
> 15-20 black peppercorns
> 1½ to 2 tablespoons salt
> 5 tablespoons tomato paste

Wash all the vegetables and chop into large pieces.

Heat oil in a roasting pan as you preheat oven to 375°F.

Spread bones over bottom of the pan and then roast for 20 minutes, stirring every five minutes. Add all the vegetables, garlic, herbs, and salt and pepper. Roast this mixture for 25 minutes, still stirring frequently. Add tomato paste and braise until the entire mixture is nicely browned, about 15 to 20 minutes more. (If tomato paste sticks to bottom of pan, add a touch of the stock.)

Transfer to a soup pot, scraping out the bottom of the roasting pan. Add stock, bring to a boil, and then simmer, uncovered, for four hours.

Strain through a fine sieve or cheesecloth. Retain only the stock. Degrease now or after refrigerating until the fat solidifies on surface.

Brown stock can be used as is, frozen, or used as the base for demi-glace or glace de viande (recipes follow).

**Glace de Viande.** Reduce strained, fat-free brown stock to approximately 3 cups by gently boiling, uncovered, for four to five hours. The resulting liquid should be thick and syrupy.

Cool to room temperature. You can store glace de viande in the refrigerator several weeks or freeze it.

**Demi-glace.** Begin as for brown stock, roasting bones and vegetables. After adding tomato paste and braising the entire mixture, sprinkle three to four tablespoons of flour over the mixture in the roasting pan and stir well.

Deglaze the pan with a small amount of red wine. Transfer everything to a soup pot, making sure not to leave anything behind in the roasting pan. Add stock, bring to a boil, and then simmer for four hours.

Strain and degrease as for brown stock.

Return to heat and reduce to 2½ to 3 quarts by gently boiling, uncovered, for several hours.

Cool to room temperature and store in refrigerator or freezer.

# fonds de Veau
# Veal Stock

*Yields 3 quarts*

*Rib and shank veal bones are the best choice for making a rich veal stock.*

4-6 pounds veal bones and trimmings
2 carrots
2 stalks celery
2 leeks, white ends only
2 onions
4-6 whole cloves
1 bunch parsley
Thyme, 1 fresh sprig or ¼ teaspoon dried
5-6 bay leaves
10-15 black peppercorns
1½ tablespoons salt

Wash vegetables (peel onions) and chop into large pieces.

Lay bones, trimmings, and vegetables in a soup pot. Pour one gallon cold water over these and bring to a boil. Skim off any scum that may rise to the surface now and later during simmering. Reduce heat and add cloves, herbs, salt, and pepper. Simmer, uncovered, for three to four hours. Correct seasonings if necessary.

Strain through a fine sieve or cheesecloth. Degrease if necessary. Refrigerate until ready to use.

fonds de Volaille
# Chicken Stock
*Yields 3 quarts*

*The entire chicken carcass—bones, back, neck, wings, skin, and innards—may be used for this chicken stock. Reduced, it produces a classic glace de volaille, given here as a variation.*

> 5-6 pounds chicken carcasses
> 2 carrots
> 3 onions, peeled
> 2 stalks celery
> 2 leeks, white part only
> 2 tablespoons salt
> 15-20 peppercorns
> 5-6 bay leaves
> Thyme, 2 sprigs fresh leaves or ½ teaspoon dried
> Basil, 4 fresh leaves or ¼ tablespoon dried
> 4 whole cloves
> 1 bunch parsley

Wash carrots, celery, and leeks; chop these and onions into large pieces. Place everything into soup pot, cover with one gallon cold water, and bring to a boil. Skim off any scum that may rise to the surface as you simmer, uncovered, for 2½ to 3 hours. Adjust seasonings. Strain through a fine sieve or cheesecloth.

Refrigerate until ready to use. Skim off the fat when cold. (You may wish to save this fat for other uses, such as in soups and sauces for chicken dishes in place of butter.)

**Glace de Volaille.** Reduce strained, fat-free chicken stock to two to three cups by simmering, uncovered, for three to four hours.

# fonds de poisson
## Fish Stock

*Yields 3 to 3 ½ quarts*

*Use whole fish carcasses, with bones, skins, heads, and scraps included, to make this clear fish stock. The eggshells are needed only if the stock is to be used to make fish aspic; they serve to clarify the liquid. Glace de poisson is the reduction of the fish stock, given here as a variation.*

    5-6 pounds fish carcasses
    2 carrots
    3 onions, peeled
    2 stalks celery
    2 leeks, white ends only
    Handful mushroom stems, optional
    2 tablespoons salt
    15-20 black peppercorns
    5-6 bay leaves
    Thyme, 2 sprigs fresh leaves or ½ teaspoon dried
    4-5 whole cloves
    1 bunch parsley
    2 cups dry white wine
    10-15 eggshells, optional

Rinse fish carcasses well under cold water. Wash carrots, celery, and leeks; chop these and onions into large pieces.

Place everything except wine into a soup pot. Bring to a boil and skim off any scum that may rise to the surface now and later during simmering. Reduce heat and add wine. Then simmer, uncovered, for about 1 ½ hours. Strain through a fine sieve or cheesecloth.

**Glace de Poisson.** Reduce strained fish stock to two to three cups by simmering, uncovered, for three to four hours.

# Soups

HOT OR COLD, clear or creamy, smooth or filled with delicious juliennes, soups are one of the most satisfying elements of a gourmet meal. "It is to a dinner what a portico or peristyle is to a building," Grimod de la Reyniere said of soup. "That is to say, it is not only the first part of it, but it must be devised in such a manner as to set the tone of the whole banquet, in the same way as the overture of an opera announces the subject of the work."

A light clear consomme can provide the perfect contrast to an elaborate entree; here again, it can be chilled to a glowing jelly, or garnished with julienne of vegetables and feather-light mousselines for a hot beginning to the meal. The velvety lobster bisque, on the other hand, made even more distinctive by the addition of lobster butter as the final step, can set off a more delicate main dish by its rich texture and flavor.

I have included in this chapter the soups that are most in demand at the Abbey. Their variety reflects their widespread places of origin, as far afield as India, France, and the American South; but they all have in common an appeal to the eye and to the palate.

## Clear Oxtail Soup
*Serves 8 to 10*

*This soup requires eggshells or egg whites in a second "clarifying" step—so save your eggshells or plan your menu around a dish (or dessert) that uses eggs or egg yolks. You can skip the clarifying when you make the thicker oxtail soup variation that follows the basic recipe.*

2 quarts beef stock (page 4)

4 tablespoons butter
1 oxtail, 2-3 pounds
1 carrot
1 stalk celery
1 leek, white end only
1 onion
⅓ cup tomato paste
1 cup dry red wine
3-4 whole cloves
6-7 juniper berries, crushed
Basil, 1 sprig fresh or ¼ teaspoon dried
5-6 bay leaves
Marjoram, 1 sprig fresh or ¼ teaspoon dried
Sage, 1 sprig fresh or ¼ teaspoon dried
Thyme, several sprigs fresh or ½ teaspoon dried
Touch freshly ground black pepper
Salt

Chop oxtail and washed, peeled vegetables into large pieces.

Melt butter in a roasting pan as you preheat oven to 375°F. Spread oxtail pieces and vegetables over bottom of the pan. Roast until oxtail is nicely browned, about 20 to 30 minutes. Stir every five minutes.

Add tomato paste and braise for 15 to 20 more minutes.

Deglaze the roasting pan with the red wine and then transfer everything to a soup pot.

Add beef stock, herbs and spices. Bring to a boil; then simmer, uncovered, until oxtail is cooked through, 1½ to 2 hours. Correct seasonings if necessary. Strain and refrigerate the liquid. (Clarifying works best when starting with a cold liquid.)

Remove meat from oxtail bones, chop, and save to add to soup later. Discard strained vegetables and herbs.

*To Clarify*

> 2 onions, halved
> Salt
> Freshly ground white pepper
> 10-15 eggshells or 5-8 egg whites
> 1 to 1½ pound lean ground beef
> 1 carrot
> 1 stalk celery
> 1 leek white end only
> ⅓ cup sherry
> Optional garnish: cooked, diced carrots, celery, mushrooms, and/or turnips

Sear the cut surfaces of the onion halves directly on a burner or in an ungreased skillet until blackened.

Chop the washed vegetables into large pieces. Place all ingredients in a soup pot, then pour in the cold oxtail stock. Mix stock thoroughly with other ingredients and bring to a boil. Simmer, uncovered, for 1½ hours. You will see that the soup has cleared.

Strain through cheesecloth. Degrease with a paper towel. Return soup to a pot and bring back to a simmer. Stir in oxtail meat, sherry, and the cooked vegetable garnish if desired. Serve immediately.

**Thickened Clear Oxtail Soup.** Prepare oxtail soup as above. During the clarification simmering (for 1½ hours), whisk in a paste of 1 to 1½ teaspoons arrowroot or cornstarch mixed first with a little sherry or red wine.

**Thickened Unclarified Oxtail Soup.** Prepare oxtail soup as above, omitting the clarifying step. After braising the tomato paste (in the roasting pan with oxtail and vegetables), sprinkle in 2 to 2½ tablespoons of flour before deglazing with the wine. After straining, return to pot and simmer, adding meat, sherry, and, if desired, cooked vegetable garnish. Serve.

## Consomme Double froid a la Russe
## Chilled Consomme with Caviar
*Serves 8*

*Whenever I serve this soup at the Abbey, I garnish it with the best Beluga Malosol caviar and accompany it with a glass of chilled imported vodka. Chilled consomme must be more strongly flavored than hot; but otherwise a hot consomme may be prepared with this same recipe and garnished with julienne of vegetables, chicken or veal quenelles, julienne of crepes, noodles, or the like.*

2 quarts good flavorful beef stock, cold (page 4)
6-8 tablespoons creme fraiche (page 49) or sour cream

2 onions, halved
1 turnip
1 carrot
1 celery stalk
2 leeks, white part only
1 pound lean ground beef
1½ pounds veal knuckles, cut into small pieces
Salt
15-18 black peppercorns

2 cloves garlic, minced
Thyme, 2 sprigs fresh or ½ teaspoon dried
5 bay leaves
Basil, 1 sprig fresh or ½ teaspoon dried
Small bunch parsley, well washed
Touch of fresh chervil, optional
10-12 eggshells or 5 egg whites
⅓ cup dry sherry

Good black Russian caviar
8 lemon slices
Fine chopped fresh chives

Sear the cut surfaces of the onion halves directly on a burner or in an ungreased skillet until blackened. Wash the other vegetables and chop into large pieces.

Place all vegetables, ground beef, veal knuckles, and all herbs and spices into a large pot. Add eggshells or egg whites and beef stock. Stir this with a large spoon so that ground beef and vegetables will not stick to the bottom of the pot. Place pot on heat, uncovered, and bring to a quick boil; then simmer for about three hours. During this time *do not stir the consomme.* (While consomme is simmering, you will notice that all the particles of the stock will simmer toward the center of the pot, and around the sides of the pot the soup will be clear and have a light golden color, like tea.) Strain very carefully through a fine sieve and then again through a strainer, lined with a white napkin or cheesecloth. Season with salt if necessary.

Skim all fat from consomme, add sherry, allow to cool, and then refrigerate until completely gelled.

When ready to serve, scoop into individual cups. Top each with a dollop of creme fraiche and a sprinkling of caviar. Garnish with sliced lemon and sprinkle with chopped chives.

Vichyssoise
# Chilled Potato and Leek Soup
*Serves 6-8*

*This classic chilled cream soup can be made with beef stock, but I prefer to use chicken stock at the Abbey.*

3-4 cups chicken stock (page 8)

6 potatoes, peeled
2 leeks, white part only, washed
1 stalk celery, washed
1 onion, peeled
Thyme, ½ sprig fresh or ¼ teaspoon dried
Touch fresh basil
3 bay leaves
1 ½ to 2 cups heavy cream
Salt
Freshly ground white pepper
1 tablespoon chopped fresh parsley or chives

Chop vegetables into large pieces; place into a soup pot and cover with stock. Add thyme, basil, and bay leaves. Boil until potatoes are done, 25 to 30 minutes.

Cool slightly; then puree in a blender or food processor. Refrigerate until cold. Blend in heavy cream and season with salt and pepper. Aim for a creamy consistency, much like creamy salad dressing. (Add more chicken stock or cream if necessary.) Refrigerate until ready to serve.

To serve, ladle soup into individual dishes and sprinkle with parsley or chives.

potage aux Grenouilles
# Cream of Frog Leg Soup
*Serves 8*

*A lovely cream soup with julienne of vegetables and the delicate meat of frog legs.*

> 3 cups chicken stock (page 8)
> ¼ cup creme fraiche (page 49)
>
> ¼ pound butter
> 2 shallots, fine chopped
> Julienne of vegetables, ¼ cup each: carrot, celery, and white part of leek
> ¼ cup diced mushrooms
> 1 clove garlic, minced
> 3 bay leaves
> 1½ cups heavy cream
> ½ cup dry white wine or dry vermouth
> Salt
> Freshly ground white pepper
> 12 frog legs
> Pinch saffron threads
> 1 tomato; peeled, seeds removed, diced, and sauteed
> ¼ cup cleaned chopped watercress
> ¼ cup cleaned julienne of sorrel
> 4-6 egg yolks

Melt a third of the butter in a soup pot. Add shallots, carrots, celery, and leek and saute for three to four minutes, until translucent but not browned. Add mushrooms, garlic, and bay leaves; cook over medium heat three to four more minutes. Add all but three tablespoons of the heavy cream. Simmering uncovered, reduce by ⅓. Stir in chicken stock and wine, season with salt and pepper, and simmer.

While soup is simmering, season frog legs with salt and pepper. Saute in a skillet in another third of the butter until done, about five or six minutes. Remove meat from the bones and cut into strips.

As soup continues to simmer, stir in saffron and tomato. Slowly add remaining butter bit by bit, whisking lightly (so as not to mash the vegetables) after each addition. Stir in creme fraiche, add watercress and sorrel, and simmer for a few more minutes.

Mix egg yolks with remaining cream. Warm this mixture by stirring in several spoonfuls of hot soup. Then slowly add this mixture back into the soup, stirring constantly. Make sure soup does not boil (and is barely simmering) as you do this. Correct seasoning if necessary.

Place frog leg strips into serving terrine, pour soup over them, and sprinkle with chives or parsley. Serve immediately.

## CReme Milanaise
# Cream of Tomato Soup
*Serves 8 to 10*

*Julienne of ham and diced macaroni are included in this classic cream of tomato soup, which is then topped with Parmesan and browned briefly.*

> 1 quart beef stock (page 4)
> ¼ cup creme fraiche (page 49
>
> ¼ cup olive oil
> ¼ pound butter
> 1 stalk celery
> ½ carrot
> 1 leek, white part only
> 1 onion, peeled and diced
> 3-4 tomatoes, cored and quartered
> 4-5 tablespoons tomato paste

2-3 garlic cloves, minced
Thyme, 1 sprig fresh or ¼ teaspoon dried
4-5 bay leaves
Oregano, 1 sprig fresh or ¼ teaspoon dried
Rosemary, few leaves fresh or ¼ teaspoon dried
1½ to 2 tablespoons flour
1 cup heavy cream
Pinch sugar
Salt
Freshly ground white pepper
3 tomatoes; peeled, seeds removed, diced and sauteed
3-4 egg yolks
½ cup cooked elbow macaroni
¼ cup cooked julienne of ham
8-10 teaspoons grated Parmesan cheese

Wash carrot, celery, and leek and chop into large pieces. Peel and dice onion. Heat olive oil and half of the butter in a soup pot over medium heat. Add vegetables and tomato quarters. Saute for five to eight minutes, or until tender but not browned. Add tomato paste, garlic, and herbs; braise for about five minutes. Sprinkle in flour and stir well. Then blend in stock and half of the heavy cream. Season with sugar, salt, and pepper. Bring to a boil; then simmer for 25 to 30 minutes, uncovered, stirring occasionally with a wire whisk.

Remove from heat and strain through a fine sieve or cheesecloth. Discard all particles. Return soup to heat, bring to a gentle boil, and whisk in the remaining butter bit by bit. Beat in creme fraiche; then add sauteed tomato pieces.

Mix remaining heavy cream with egg yolks. Remove soup from heat and stir this mixture slowly into the soup. To thicken, return to lowest heat and whisk for about two more minutes, but do not let the soup boil or even simmer any more.

To serve, divide macaroni among individual serving dishes, add julienne of ham, and pour soup over this. Sprinkle with Parmesan cheese, broil until lightly browned, and serve.

# Chicken Mulligatawny

*Serves 6 to 8*

*I developed this recipe when I was a chef in South Africa with its large Indian population. This version is different from the creamy mulligatawny that one often encounters, and I think it is excellent. Be sure to use real imported Madras curry powder for the best results.*

3 cups chicken stock (page 8)

2 tomatoes

Julienne of vegetables, ¼ cup each: carrot, celery, white end of leek

¼ cup fine-chopped onion

2 tablespoons butter

2 teaspoons Madras curry powder

1 tablespoon flour

2 cloves garlic, minced

Touch coriander

Touch ginger, freshly grated

Salt

Freshly ground white pepper

¼ cup cooked rice

1 teaspoon mango chutney, optional for light sweetness

2 tablespoons chopped chives

Place the chicken stock and chicken into a large pot and bring to a boil. Reduce heat and simmer until chicken is done, about 30 to 45 minutes. Strain; reserve chicken and stock. Cool chicken enough to remove meat from bones. Reserve amount of meat desired for soup. (The rest can be used for something else, such as chicken salad.)

Peel tomatoes, remove seeds, dice, and saute. Set aside.

In a soup pot, saute julienne of vegetables and onions in butter. Sprinkle with curry powder and flour; mix well. Add garlic, coriander, ginger, and reserved stock; season with salt and pepper. Bring to a boil; then simmer for 15 minutes. Stir in sauteed tomatoes, rice, chicken pieces, and mango chutney (if desired). Simmer for five more minutes. Correct seasonings to taste. Serve sprinkled with chives.

## Soupe aux moules a l'abbe
## Mussel Soup of the Abbey
*Serves 4 to 6*

*To make the broth for this delicious mussel cream soup you should have a covered pan big enough to steam the mussels in as they lie flat on the bottom. I prefer to use vermouth in the stock.*

¼ cup creme fraiche (page 49)

5 tablespoons butter
3-4 shallots, chopped fine
1 clove garlic, minced
9-10 bay leaves
1 bunch parsley
Juice from 1-2 lemons
1 cup vermouth or dry white wine
2 pounds mussels, well washed and all sand removed

Julienne of vegetables, ¼ cup each: carrots, celery, leeks
   (white ends only)
¼ cup diced mushrooms
1 pint heavy cream
Fine-chopped parsley
Salt
Freshly ground white pepper
Pinch saffron
4-6 egg yolks

## To prepare broth

Melt a tablespoon of the butter in your chosen pan. Add shallots (reserve ¼ cup for later) and garlic and gently saute for three to four minutes until translucent, but not browned. Add 5-6 bay leaves, the bunch of parsley, lemon juice, vermouth, and one cup of water. Boil for two to three minutes.

Spread mussels over the bottom of the pan in one layer. Cover and steam until mussels open, about three to five minutes. Remove from heat and transfer mussels to a dish. *Discard any closed mussels*. Strain broth carefully through cheesecloth so that no sand remains in the stock; save this stock.

When mussels are cool enough to handle, take them out of the shell and remove their black rims. Reserve a few mussels in the shell—they will later garnish the soup. Also, save the empty shells for the same purpose.

## To finish soup

In a soup pot, saute carrots, celery, leeks, and reserved shallots in two tablespoons of the butter for three to five minutes. Do not brown the vegetables. Reduce heat to medium, add mushrooms and remaining bay leaves, and cook for two to three more minutes. Pour in two-thirds of the heavy cream and slowly simmer, uncovered, until reduced by one-third, about ten minutes.

Add saved mussel stock, some chopped parsley, saffron, and salt and pepper to taste. Simmer, uncovered, for five to ten minutes.

While soup is simmering, place mussels into serving terrine. Mix egg yolks with remaining heavy cream.

Stir remaining butter into soup. Let simmer five more minutes, stirring occasionally. Stir in creme fraiche. Remove soup from heat.

Spoon some hot soup slowly into egg yolks and cream. Then

stir this warmed mixture back into soup. Return to low heat and stir until hot, but do not boil.

Pour soup over mussels in tureen. Add a few mussels in the shells to the soup. Use empty shells for decoration around the tureen. Sprinkle with parsley and serve immediately.

## new Orleans Style Seafood Gumbo

*Serves 6 to 8*

*There are as many "New Orleans" gumbos as there are chefs, and this is my own favorite. Gumbo file is a powder made from young sassafras leaves, used to thicken the traditional Lousiana gumbos. A variety of fresh fish may be used in this gumbo, according to what is locally available.*

> 3 cups fish stock (page 9)
> 1¼ to 1½ pounds fresh fish: cod, halibut, shrimp, crabmeat, scallops, snapper, etc.
> 1 stalk celery, diced
> 1 onion, peeled and diced
> ¼ pound butter
> 1½ to 2 tablespoons flour
> 1 cup dry white wine
> 1 cup heavy cream
> 2 cloves garlic, minced
> 3 bay leaves
> Thyme leaves, 1 sprig fresh or ¼ teaspoon dried
> ½ teaspoon gumbo file
> Pinch cayenne pepper
> Salt to taste
> Freshly ground white pepper
> 2 tomatoes, peeled, seeds removed, diced, and sauteed
> 1 bell pepper, diced and sauteed
> ⅓ cup chopped cooked okra, washed thoroughly to remove any slippery coating
> 3 egg yolks

Cut fish into 1½ to 2 inch pieces. Bring fish stock to a boil. Add fish and simmer for five to eight minutes. Remove fish from stock and set aside. Remove fish stock.

Saute celery and onion in half of the butter for three to five minutes, but do not brown. Reduce heat, add flour, and stir well. Slowly pour in fish stock, white wine, and half of the cream, stirring constantly to prevent lumping. Stir in garlic, herbs, and spices; season with salt and pepper. Simmer for 20-25 minutes, uncovered. Whisk in remaining butter, bit by bit, as soup continues to simmer. Add prepared tomatoes, bell pepper, and okra. Mix remaining cream with egg yolks and slowly stir into soup. Keep stirring on lowest heat for about two minutes, but do not boil or even simmer any more. Correct seasonings if needed.

Add fish and serve immediately.

## Bisque δε homarδ
## Lobster Cream Soup

*Serves 6 to 8*

*The velvety texture of this lobster bisque comes from whipping in the butter at the very last. If you have lobster butter on hand, use it instead to achieve a more distinct lobster flavor.*

1 pint chicken stock (page 8)
1 pint fish stock (page 9)
½ cup creme fraiche (page 49)

1 celery stalk
1 carrot
1 onion
1 leek, white part only
¼ cup chopped mushroom stems, optional
3 lobster tails with shells
6-8 lobster shells
¼ pound butter
⅓ cup tomato paste
2-3 tablespoons flour
½ cup heavy cream
Salt to taste
Freshly ground white pepper to taste
4-5 bay leaves
Thyme, 1 sprig fresh or ½ teaspoon dried
Basil, ½ sprig fresh or ¼ teaspoon dried
2 garlic cloves, minced
½ teaspoon saffron threads
2 tablespoons cognac
2 tablespoons dry sherry
Pinch of cayenne
3 egg yolks
2 teaspoons fine-chopped fresh chives

Cut lobster tails and shells into large pieces. Wash celery, carrot, and leek and chop into large pieces. Peel onion and quarter.

Saute all vegetables, lobster tails, and lobster shells in half of the butter for 10 to 15 minutes. Add tomato paste and braise for about five minutes more, stirring to keep mixture from sticking to the bottom of the pot. Add flour, mix well, then add half of the heavy cream, and the chicken and fish stock. Season with salt and pepper; add bay leaves, thyme, basil, garlic, and saffron. Stir well and simmer for 45 minutes, stirring frequently.

Remove from heat and strain soup through a fine sieve or cheesecloth. Discard vegetables, but save lobster tails. Return soup to heat and bring to a boil. Reduce to simmer, and add cognac, sherry, and cayenne. While stirring, add bits of the remaining fresh butter, a few at a time. Mix in creme fraiche.

While the soup is simmering, remove the shells from the lobster tails and dice the meat finely. Discard all shells. Mix egg yolks with the remaining cream. Remove soup from heat and gradually whisk in egg yolk and cream mixture. To thicken, return to lowest heat, and stir well for one minute, but do not boil or simmer. Strain soup again.

Pour soup over lobster meat in serving terrine and sprinkle with fresh chives. Serve immediately.

# Sauces
# and Butters

HE SAUCES THAT I PREPARE to serve with so many of the dishes we serve at the Abbey have perhaps done more than any other single factor to establish our reputation in the world of food. Some are classic sauces, some are original, some are served hot, some cold; but all have this in common: their purpose is to complement a dish, to bring out its subtle flavor and to add to it in ways that can be gloriously variable. "You don't often find this type of sauce in the United States," the great chef Roger Verge commented when he ate at the Abbey.

The nouvelle cuisine that has been introduced within the last decade in many of the best kitchens has, it is true, altered the nature of many of the sauces I prepare. My sauces now are lighter, using just as much butter and eggs as they always have but being thickened with very little starch, if any. Instead, the sauce will be simmered until it is reduced and thickened; or it will be thickened with pureed vegetables, with goose liver pate, with reduced cream or with creme fraiche. It is obvious that the sauces of the nouvelle cuisine, while they are lighter to the palate, are just as calorie-laden as the more floury sauces they have replaced!

There are times, I believe, when a little flour is a more appropriate thickener for a sauce; and so my kitchen combines the best of the old cuisine with the best of the new. Depending on the dish for which it is intended, a sauce may be prepared in one of several manners; and the recipes I will include here take this into account. Many sauces may be prepared ahead and even frozen; but I do not recommend freezing either egg-and-cream sauces or white cream sauces for later use, as they tend to separate.

The basis of all my brown sauces is the *demi-glace* prepared from the brown stock; and the basis for all my white sauces is the clear stock from fish, chicken, veal, or even beef. In most cases, though, the sauce is prepared especially for a particular dish; and so, of course, the drippings, bones, and liquid from that dish will be used in the preparation of the sauce, to give it a richer flavor. So the fish stock to which one adds shallots, wine, lemon, and butter and which one uses as poaching liquid can be strained after the fish is ready and used immediately as the basis for its sauce. And the bones from a roasting pheasant or veal can be simmered with a clear stock at the last minute to share their own distinctive flavors with those of the complementary sauce.

Do not neglect to *deglaze* the pan in which you have sauteed or roasted your main dish; it is an essential step to making a fine sauce. After you have drained the excess grease from the pan, simply add stock, wine, or a previously prepared basic sauce, scrape off the small bits of food that have stuck to the pan, and simmer it briefly; this allows you to retain the essential flavors of the pan juices and crisp fragments.

Egg-and-butter sauces such as hollandaise, on the other hand, require only simple, fresh ingredients and a sure hand to prepare, though their variations are many and delightful. The home chef will often find it useful to prepare these in a blender; indeed, even at the Abbey we use a large mixer in order to be able to prepare these sauces in the quantities we need. In the end, it is experience that teaches best when such a sauce is perfect. It would horrify some chefs to see me prepare hollandaise over a direct flame; but years of making the sauce have taught me just when I must remove it from the fire. Remember that an egg-and-butter sauce does not keep well; prepare it shortly before you need it and keep it warm, not chilled.

Among my favorite sauces are the cold sauces that use mayonnaise as their base; I have included several that are original to the Abbey, as well as my own variations on more classic recipes. Then, I have presented a few butter mixtures, to place on grilled steak or fish, or to use instead of plain butter in the final preparation of a sauce, in order to whip in a velvety texture and a dash of additional flavor. Finally, I have included some of the Abbey's most popular dressings or dips for salads and cold vegetables.

BeuRRe Blanc
# Hot Butter Sauce
*Yields 3½ cups*

*A hot sauce made of wine, vinegar, and shallots bound with butter. Absolutely excellent with poached salmon, grilled trout, or almost any good seafood.*

3-4 shallots, chopped fine
¾ cup white wine vinegar
⅔ cup dry white wine
¾ to 1 pound butter, cut in small pieces and kept cold
Salt
Freshly ground white pepper

Mix shallots, vinegar, and wine in a small saucepan (enamel works best), and boil over medium heat until it is reduced to a syrupy consistency. (Liquid will be almost totally evaporated.) Remove from heat and let cool slightly.

Return to a very low heat. Whisk in butter quickly, piece by piece. After all the butter is incorporated, the warm sauce should have the consistency of a mayonnaise. Season with salt and white pepper, and serve at once.

## Sauce Bordelaise

*Yields 6 cups*

*True bordelaise sauce is made with marrow, either ground fine and added to the sauce to flavor it, or diced and poached and then added to the finished sauce. Your butcher can cut the bone so that the marrow can be removed intact; or you can poach the bone and remove it afterwards.*

> 5 cups demi-glace (page 6)
>
> 3-4 shallots, chopped fine
> 6 tablespoons butter
> 2 cups dry red wine
> Juice from ½ lemon
> Touch cayenne
> Salt
> Freshly ground black pepper
> ¼ to ½ pound marrow, diced

Saute shallots in half of the butter in a large saucepan. Cook only until tender, not browned.

Add wine, demi-glace, lemon juice, cayenne; season with salt and pepper.

Boil gently to reduce sauce to consistency of demi-glace originally.

While sauce is boiling, blanch diced marrow for two to three minutes in a small amount of boiling water. Drain and set aside.

Whisk remaining butter, bit by bit, into boiling sauce. Correct seasoning if necessary. Stir in blanched marrow and serve. (If not serving immediately, keep warm and add marrow just before serving).

Bordelaise sauce can be refrigerated and reheated.

SAUCE AU POIVRE VERT
# Green Peppercorn Sauce
*Yields 1 quart*

*This strongly flavored sauce combines the tastes of green peppercorns and cognac. It goes well with almost any beef dish.*

> 1 quart demi-glace (page 6)
>
> 6 tablespoons butter
> 2-3 shallots, chopped fine
> Thyme, 1 spring fresh or ¼ teaspoon dried
> 4 bay leaves
> 3-4 tablespoons green peppercorns, packed in vinegar
> ½ to 1 tablespoon tomato paste
> ½ cup dry white wine
> Salt
> Freshly ground black pepper
> ¼ cup cognac

Melt half of the butter in a large saucepan. Add shallots, thyme, bay leaves, half of the peppercorns, and a touch of the peppercorn juice. Cook over medium heat for three to five minutes.

Add tomato paste and braise two or three minutes. Add demi-glace and wine and boil until sauce has the same consistency as the demi-glace originally. Add salt and pepper to taste.

Strain, then return to heat. Bring to a gentle boil; then whisk in remaining butter bit by bit. Stir in remaining peppercorns and cognac.

Serve immediately or keep warm. This sauce can also be refrigerated and reheated.

## Sauce ∂'agneau
## Lamb Sauce
*Yields 6 to 6½ cups*

*A lighter sauce flavored with thyme, rosemary, and garlic, which begins with lamb bones and combines with a basic brown stock. Have your butcher chop three- to four-inch lengths of bone from the rib, loin, or shank. We serve this sauce with our saddle of lamb in puff pastry, but it could be served with any lamb dish.*

1 quart demi-glace (page 6)
2 cups beef stock (page 4)

4 tablespoons butter
4 pounds lamb bones
1 carrot
1 stalk celery
1 leek, white end only
2 onions, peeled
1 tablespoon tomato paste
⅓ cup Madeira wine
2 cloves garlic, minced
Thyme, several sprigs fresh or ½ teaspoon dried
5-6 bay leaves
Rosemary, 1 sprig fresh or ¼ teaspoon dried
Salt
Freshly ground black pepper

Wash carrot, celery, and leek; dice these and the onions. Melt butter in a roasting pan in the oven as it preheats to 375°F. Add bones and vegetables and roast, stirring frequently, until bones are lightly browned, about 30 minutes. Add tomato paste and braise for about 15 minutes more, still stirring often.

Deglaze roasting pan with Madeira, then transfer everything to a soup pot. Add garlic and herbs and season with salt and pepper. Pour demi-glace and beef stock over all. Bring to a boil, then reduce to simmer for 1½ to 2 hours. Adjust seasonings if necessary.

Strain, then skim off fat or refrigerate until solidified enough to remove. Keep warm until serving or refrigerate and reheat.

## Paprika Cream Sauce
*Yields 7 cups*

*Neither a brown nor a white sauce, this delicious sauce with its strong paprika flavor can be served with chicken, veal, or lamb. Use the appropriate stock in the recipe according to which dish it will accompany.*

2 cups demi-glace (page 6)
2 cups chicken, veal, or beef stock (pages 4, 7, 8)
¼ cup creme fraiche  (page 49)

5 tablespoons butter
¼ pound bacon, uncooked
2-3 chopped shallots or 1 large chopped onion
4-5 tablespoons Hungarian paprika
1½ to 2 tablespoons tomato paste
1 to 1½ tablespoons flour
Juice from 1 lemon
1 clove garlic, minced
5-6 bay leaves
½ cup dry white wine
¼ cup heavy cream
Salt
Freshly ground white pepper

Melt half of the butter in a large saucepan. Add bacon and saute until translucent. Add shallots and cook for three to five minutes more over medium heat, also until translucent, but not browned.

Remove pan from heat and mix in paprika and tomato paste. Sprinkle in flour and mix again. Pour in demi-glace and stock; add lemon juice, garlic, bay leaves, white wine, and heavy cream. Return to heat.

While stirring continuously, bring to a boil. Reduce heat and simmer for 15 to 20 minutes. Add salt and pepper to taste. Strain through a fine mesh sieve or cheesecloth.

Return again to heat and bring to a boil. Whisk in remaining butter bit by bit. Stir in creme fraiche; continue to boil gently for two more minutes. Serve immediately or keep warm until serving.

This sauce can be refrigerated for several days and reheated. Freezing is not recommended.

Sauce Chasseur
# Hunter Sauce
*Yields 5 cups*

*A red wine sauce served with many beef dishes, this sauce includes diced peeled tomatoes, tomato paste, and mushrooms.*

> 1 quart demi-glace (page 6)
> 2 shallots, chopped fine
> 5 tablespoons butter
> 1 clove garlic, minced
> 1 cup sliced fresh mushrooms
> 2-3 bay leaves
> 3 medium tomatoes, peeled and diced
> 1 tablespoon tomato paste
> ½ cup dry red wine
> Salt
> Freshly ground pepper
> 2 tablespoons chopped parsley

In a large saucepan, saute shallots in half of the butter until translucent. Add garlic, mushrooms, and bay leaves; saute for three to four minutes more. Add tomatoes and saute only briefly. Stir in tomato paste and braise for one to two minutes. Add red wine and demi-glace. Bring to a gentle boil, then whip in remaining butter bit by bit. Season with salt and pepper and sprinkle with parsley. Stir and serve.

## Sauce Bourguignonne
## Burgundy Sauce

*Yields 5 cups*

*A classic sauce that takes only a few minutes to prepare, using the bones and drippings from the dish you are preparing, and combining them with Burgundy and demi-glace. I substitute maitre d'hotel butter (page 55) for the butter in this recipe, for a distinctive difference. Two good variations of this sauce are the champignon sauce, which uses fresh mushrooms, and Madeira sauce, which substitutes Madeira wine for the Burgundy.*

> 1 quart demi-glace (page 6)
>
> 3-4 shallots, chopped fine
> 1-2 cloves garlic, chopped fine
> 5 tablespoons butter
> 1 cup Burgundy wine
> Salt
> Freshly ground black pepper

Saute shallots and garlic in two tablespoons of the butter until translucent, but not browned.

Add Burgundy, demi-glace, and salt and pepper to taste. Bring to a boil; then whisk in remaining butter bit by bit.

Serve immediately or keep warm until serving.

This sauce can be refrigerated and reheated.

**Sauce Champignon.** Prepare as for Sauce Bourguignonne, but add ½ to 1 pound sliced fresh mushrooms to shallots and garlic. A white Burgundy can be substituted for a lighter variation.

**Sauce Madeira.** Prepare as for Sauce Bourguignonne, but use a good Madeira wine in place of Burgundy.

## Sauce Moutarde
# Mustard Sauce

*Yields 6 to 6½ cups*

*Whether you are preparing this creamy brown sauce for tournedos or pepper steaks, the flavors in your drippings will combine with shallots and smooth brown prepared mustard to produce a sharp, tangy contrast. I use Dusseldorf mustard, good and commonly available. The shallots are not strained out of the sauce. The addition of green peppercorns makes a nice variation on this recipe.*

> 1 quart demi-glace (page 6)
> ½ cup creme fraiche (page 49)
>
> ¼ pound butter
> 3 shallots, chopped fine
> 1 clove garlic, minced
> 4-5 bay leaves
> 4-5 tablespoons brown, seedless mustard
> ½ cup heavy cream
> ½ cup dry white wine
> Salt
> Freshly ground white pepper

Melt half of the butter in a large saucepan. Add shallots, garlic, and bay leaves and cook gently for three to five minutes. Do not brown the mixture.

Add mustard and braise for two minutes. Pour in heavy cream and reduce to half the original volume by boiling gently, uncovered, for about 15 minutes.

Stir in white wine and demi-glace. Bring to a boil, then boil gently for five minutes. Reduce heat to simmer and whisk in remaining butter bit by bit.

Stir in creme fraiche and season with salt and pepper. Bring back to a boil, then serve.

Sauce Moutarde can also be refrigerated and reheated (boiled again) when needed.

**Green Peppercorn Sauce.** Prepare as for Sauce Moutarde. When sauce is ready, add four tablespoons green peppercorns (packed in brine, not in vinegar) and a touch of the brine to taste, and boil for three to four minutes.

### Sauce Bigarade
## Orange Sauce
*Yields 2½ to 3 cups*

*A sweet orange sauce for duck, made with demi-glace and Grand Marnier or Cointreau, and with a strong flavor of currant jelly. Save your duck carcass and the pan juices; they are an important part of the sauce.*

⅓ cup demi-glace (page 6)

1 tablespoon fine julienne of orange rind
½ cup dry red wine
1 tablespoon sugar
¼ cup wine vinegar
Juice from ½ lemon
Juice from 3 oranges
2 tablespoons red currant jelly
Bones from roasted duckling, chopped into 2-inch pieces
Juice from roasted duckling
Arrowroot or cornstarch
3 tablespoons orange liqueur

Simmer julienne of orange rind in a touch of the red wine. Set aside to be added to the sauce at the last moment.

In the bottom of a large sauce pan, brown sugar very lightly, stirring so that it does not burn. Deglaze with vinegar and red wine, then add the lemon and orange juice. Boil for four to five minutes. Add demi-glace, red currant jelly, bones, and drippings. Bring to a boil, reduce heat, and simmer for 15 to 20 minutes.

Strain the sauce through a fine mesh sieve. Return to a sauce pan and bring to a simmer. Thicken slightly by mixing a small amount of arrowroot and cold liquid (water or red wine) and drizzling this, while stirring, into the sauce. Stir in orange liqueur and prepared julienne of orange rind. Keep warm until serving.

## Sauce δe Chevreuil au Poivre Vert
## Venison Green Peppercorn Sauce
*Yields 2 quarts*

*This creamy brown sauce starts with venison bones, which you can ask your butcher to prepare for you. Its distinction arises from the delicate flavor of whole green peppercorns combined with the barest hint of red currant jelly and crushed juniper berries. I prefer to use the green peppercorns canned in brine rather than in vinegar, and to use the same wine in the sauce as will be served with dinner.*

1 quart demi-glace (page 6)
2 cups beef and/or veal stock (pages 4, 7)
½ cup creme fraiche

¼ pound butter
½ pound bacon
4 pounds venison bones, cut into 2-inch lengths, and
    trimmings
1 carrot, chopped
1 stalk celery, chopped
1 leek, white end, chopped

2 onions, peeled and chopped
1½ tablespoons crushed juniper berries
5-6 bay leaves
3-4 tablespoons green peppercorns, in brine
2 tablespoons tomato paste
1 cup dry red wine
½ cup heavy cream
2 tablespoons red currant jelly
Juice from 1 lemon
Salt
Freshly ground black pepper

In a roasting pan, melt half of the butter as you heat the oven to 375°F. Spread bones, any trimmings, and bacon over the bottom of the pan. Roast for 30 minutes, stirring frequently.

Add all of the vegetables, juniper berries, bay leaves, and half of the green peppercorns. Continue to roast until bones are nicely browned, about 15 minutes more. Stir often during this roasting.

Add tomato paste and braise for 15 more minutes. Deglaze the roasting pan with red wine and transfer everything to a soup pot.

Add demi-glace and stock, and bring to a boil. Then simmer for about two hours.

Strain and skim off fat or refrigerate until fat solidifies enough to remove. Return to a soup pot and bring to a boil.

Stir in heavy cream, red currant jelly, and lemon juice. Continue to boil gently for three to five minutes. Then strain through cheesecloth. Bring to a boil once more and whisk in remaining butter bit by bit. Add the remaining green peppercorns and a touch of their brine. Stir in creme fraiche. Season with salt and pepper.

Keep warm until ready to serve. Venison sauce can also be refrigerated and reheated. Freezing is not recommended.

# Sauce δe tomate
## Tomato Sauce
*Yields 2 quarts*

*The choice of stock to use in this basic tomato sauce will depend on the dish with which you will use it. Olive oil and bacon add a subtle difference to the fresh tomato and herb taste of the sauce, which is thickened with a little flour. This sauce can be used with a wide variety of dishes; at the Abbey we serve it with pork medallions milanaise.*

1 quart beef or chicken stock (pages 4, 8)

¼ cup olive oil
¼ cup fine-chopped raw bacon
1 stalk celery with leaves
1 leek, white part only
1 carrot
¼ cup tomato paste
1 tablespoon flour
Thyme, 2 springs fresh or ½ teaspoon dried
3 bay leaves
Basil, 4 fresh leaves or ¼ teaspoon dried
Oregano, 1 sprig fresh or ½ teaspoon dried
1 small bunch parsley, washed
2 garlic cloves, minced
½ teaspoon sugar
Freshly ground white pepper
Salt
2 tablespoons butter
1 sweet white onion
8 medium tomatoes

Wash celery, leek, and carrot and chop into large pieces.

Heat olive oil in a large saucepan. Add bacon and vegetables and saute for eight to ten minutes. Add tomato paste and braise three to five minutes, stirring frequently. Sprinkle in flour and mix well. Stir in beef or chicken stock, herbs, garlic, and sugar; season with salt and pepper. Bring to a boil, then reduce heat and simmer for 30 minutes, stirring occasionally.

While sauce is simmering, melt butter in a large saucepan. Peel and slice onion and add with two tablespoons water. Cook, covered, over low heat until onions are soft, but not browned. Quarter tomatoes, removing core and seeds. Then add tomatoes and cook for five or six minutes, or until tomatoes are soft. Cool slightly; then puree in a food processor or blender.

Now strain your sauce through a fine sieve or cheesecloth, then mix it with the tomato and onion puree. Simmer for five to eight more minutes. Season to taste. This sauce stores well in either refrigerator or freezer.

Sauce Bechamel
# Rich Cream Sauce
*Yields 5 cups*

*This is a classic thick sauce used with a variety of dishes; unlike the veloute sauce, it is not prepared with stock. Bechamel sauce was originally made with milk and thickened with a white roux. The nouvelle cuisine, however, prefers a thinner sauce; and Bechamel is not made so frequently now. When I do make it, I use cream instead of milk and cut down on the amount of flour.*

¼ pound butter
½ cup chopped onions or shallots
3 tablespoons flour
1 quart heavy cream, warmed
Freshly grated nutmeg
Salt
Freshly ground white pepper

Melt two-thirds of the butter in a large saucepan. Add onions and saute for three to four minutes, until translucent, but not browned. Whisk in flour and blend well.

Reduce heat to low. Slowly pour in the warmed cream, whisking continuously to ensure a smooth sauce.

Increase heat slightly. Stir in a sprinkling of nutmeg, salt, and pepper. Simmer for 15 to 20 minutes, stirring frequently to prevent sauce from burning.

Then whisk in remaining butter, bit by bit. Correct seasonings if necessary. Strain.

Serve now or refrigerate and rewarm slowly in a double boiler. Do not freeze.

## Sauce Veloutee
## Velvety White Sauce
*Yields 5½ to 6 cups*

*The velvety white veloute sauce is essentially a roux, with the appropriate stock added for each individual dish. For chicken fricassee, for example, it would be made with chicken stock; and for blanquette of veal one would use the liquid from the preparation of the veal.*

> 3 cups heated chicken, fish, veal, or beef stock
>    (page 4, 7, 8, 9)
> ½ cup creme fraiche (page 49)
>
> 2-3 shallots, chopped fine
> 7 tablespoons butter
> 2-3 tablespoons flour
> ½ cup dry white wine
> 1 cup heavy cream
> Salt
> Freshly ground white pepper
> 3 egg yolks

In a large saucepan saute shallots in half of the butter until tender, but not browned. Sprinkle in flour and stir well.

Add stock, wine, half of the heavy cream; season with salt and pepper. Bring to a boil, reduce heat, and simmer 20 to 30 minutes, stirring frequently.

Strain, return to pan, and bring back to a boil. Whisk in remaining butter bit by bit. Blend in creme fraiche. Remove from heat.

If planning to refrigerate and reheat, stop here. Later, warm sauce before proceeding.

Lightly beat egg yolks with remaining cream. Spoon some hot sauce slowly into egg mixture, then stir this warmed mixture slowly back into sauce.

Return sauce to lowest heat. Keep warm until serving, but do not boil.

## Sauce Bearnaise

*Yields 2 cups*

*This famous sauce will be useful in dozens of gourmet dishes; but I also use its variation, sauce choron, which has a lovely color and flavor added by the use of tomato paste. Either can be served with meats; or I sometimes add tarragon and serve it with fish. Do not plan to make these sauces ahead of time; they are best made just before serving.*

> 2 teaspoons warm glace de viande (page 6)
>
> ½ cup dry white wine
> ¼ cup tarragon vinegar
> 1 tablespoon chopped shallots
> Salt
> ½ teaspoon crushed black or white peppercorns
> 3 tablespoons fine-chopped fresh tarragon
> 6 egg yolks
> 1 pound warm, melted butter
> Juice from ½ lemon
> Parsley, ½ teaspoon fine-chopped fresh or ¼ teaspoon
>     dried

In a small saucepan combine wine, vinegar, shallots, salt, peppercorns, and half of the tarragon. Bring to a boil, then reduce to a third of the original volume by simmering. Strain and reserve liquid.

Whisk this liquid slowly into the egg yolks in a ceramic, glass, or stainless steel bowl. Then set bowl into a double boiler over medium to high heat and whisk continuously until it thickens to a smooth consistency. Do not let eggs curdle.

Lower the heat; then drizzle in the warm, melted butter gradually, whisking constantly. After all the butter has been incorporated, remove bowl from double boiler.

Stir in lemon juice. Strain sauce. Add remaining tarragon, parsley, and warmed glace de viande. Keep warm, not hot (could separate) until serving.

Do not refrigerate and reheat.

**Sauce Choron.** Prepare bearnaise as above, but substitute a tablespoon of tomato paste for the glace de viande.

## Sauce de homard
## Lobster Cream Sauce
*Yields 5 cups*

*A heavy sauce, similar to lobster bisque but thicker. I use lobster butter at the final step, to add a velvety texture and a sharper lobster flavor. There will be plenty of lobster meat left after you strain the sauce, and you can use this later in lobster bisque.*

2 cups chicken stock (page 8)
2 cups fish stock (page 9)
½ cup bechamel sauce (page 43)
¼ cup hollandaise sauce (page 48), optional
½ cup creme fraiche (page 49)

1 celery stalk
1 carrot
1 onion, peeled
1 leek, white part only
¼ cup chopped mushroom stems, optional

3 lobster tails in shells
6-8 lobster shells
¼ pound butter
⅓ cup tomato paste
3-4 tablespoons flour
½ cup heavy cream
2 cloves garlic, minced
4-5 bay leaves
Thyme, 1 sprig fresh or ½ teaspoon dried
Basil, ½ sprig fresh or ¼ teaspoon dried
Salt
Freshly ground white pepper
½ teaspoon saffron threads
2 tablespoons cognac
Pinch of cayenne

Wash carrot, celery, and leek; chop these and onion, lobster tails, and lobster shells in large pieces.

Saute all vegetables and lobster tails and shells in half of the butter over medium heat for ten to fifteen minutes. Add tomato paste and cook for about five minutes more, stirring to keep mixture from sticking to the bottom of the pot.

Sprinkle in flour and mix well. Then stir in heavy cream and chicken and fish stocks. Add garlic and herbs; season with salt and pepper. Blend well and simmer for 45 minutes, stirring frequently.

Remove from heat and strain through a fine sieve or cheesecloth. Save tail meat for use in another dish. Return sauce to heat and bring to a simmer. Add saffron, then whisk in the remaining butter bit by bit. Simmer for ten more minutes. Stir in creme fraiche, cognac, and cayenne, then bechamel sauce. Mix well, bring to a good boil, strain again, and blend in optional hollandaise sauce.

# Sauce hollandaise

*Yields 3 cups*

*The worcestershire sauce in this hollandaise gives it a special flavor. As a sauce for salmon, it is particularly good with the addition of a little fresh tarragon. A delicious variation is sauce mousseline, which has whipped cream folded into it. Sauce maltaise is another fine variation using the juice of blood oranges; it is excellent with asparagus and is used in veal mandarin.*

> 4 tablespoons water
> 2 tablespoons white vinegar
> Touch salt
> 12 white or black peppercorns
> 6 egg yolks
> 1 pound warm melted butter
> Touch worcestershire sauce
> Juice from 2 lemons

In a small saucepan, combine water, vinegar, salt and peppercorns. Bring to a boil, then reduce over medium heat to one-third the original volume. Strain and set broth aside to cool. Discard peppercorns.

Lightly beat egg yolks and one tablespoon cold water in a stainless steel bowl set into a double boiler. Add the reserved broth and whisk the mixture over simmering water until it begins to thicken.

Drizzle in the warm butter, whisking continuously. If sauce seems too thick, add a touch of warm water. Remove from heat and stir in worcestershire sauce and lemon juice.

Serve immediately or keep warm over warm water. Hollandaise sauce may separate if it gets too hot. Do not refrigerate and reheat this sauce.

Note: The thickened egg mixture (before butter added) can be put into a blender on lowest speed and the butter drizzled in through the top.

**Sauce Mousseline.** Prepare Sauce Hollandaise as directed. Fold one cup stiffly whipped cream into the sauce. Adding some chopped fresh tarragon is also suggested. Either way, this is a good choice for poached fish.

**Sauce Maltaise.** Prepare as for Sauce Hollandaise, but keep it very thick during the whisking stage. When sauce is complete add the strained juice of three blood oranges and a touch of tomato catsup for color and sweetness.

## Creme Fraiche
*Yields 1 cup*

*Creme fraiche, a staple in France, is just starting to be available in your grocery store. All too often, though, you'll find it necessary to make it yourself. It appears in dozens of recipes in this book and it is easy to make and store.*

    1 cup heavy cream
    3 teaspoons buttermilk

Mix cream and buttermilk in a covered jar or plastic container. Shake well for a full minute. Let sit at room temperature for at least 12 hours, then store in the refrigerator. It will keep four to five weeks.

# mayonnaise

*Yields 5 cups*

*What makes my mayonnaise different is the dash of worcestershire sauce I add. Remember that all ingredients must be at room temperature before you begin. A wire whip is the best choice for making mayonnaise, but I have no objections to making it in a blender at its lowest speed. Do not use a food processor, though; the cutting blades will ruin the mayonnaise.*

    1 tablespoon salt
    8-10 egg yolks
    Juice from 1 lemon
    1 tablespoon wine vinegar
    Touch sugar
    Touch brown seedless mustard
    Touch freshly ground white pepper
    Pinch Hungarian paprika, optional
    Dash worcestershire sauce
    1 quart good vegetable oil

Add salt to egg yolks in a bowl and beat until foamy. Stir in all other ingredients except oil.

Whisking constantly, drizzle in oil in a slow, but steady, stream. If mayonnaise becomes too thick, add a touch of warm water.

# Curry Cream Mayonnaise

*Yields 1¾ cups*

*A strong cold curry sauce that is delicious served with a stuffed avocado or cold seafood. Tomato catsup adds a little sweetness, worcestershire sauce and lemon give a stronger flavor, and cream makes it especially smooth. Use only imported Madras curry powder for the best results.*

¾ cup mayonnaise (page 50)
¼ cup creme fraiche (page 49)

2-3 teaspoons Madras curry powder
3 tablespoons tomato catsup
⅓ cup heavy cream
Juice from 1-2 lemons
Salt to taste
Freshly ground white pepper to taste
Touch worcestershire sauce
2 tablespoons fine-chopped parsley

Place mayonnaise into a bowl and add all the other ingredients. Mix with a wire whip until sauce is smooth. Refrigerate until needed.

# Marie-Louise Sauce

*Yields 2 cups*

*I invented this pink cocktail sauce to serve with shrimp
cocktail or cold lobster. Essentially, it is a mayonnaise with
the addition of tomato catsup, horseradish, and cognac. I add
a touch of grapefruit juice and serve it with an appetizer of
shrimp and grapefruit sections.*

> 1½ cups mayonnaise (page 50)
> ½ cup creme fraiche (page 49)
>
> 4-5 tablespoons tomato catsup
> ¼ cup heavy cream
> 2 tablespoons prepared horseradish
> Juice of 1-2 lemons
> Grapefruit juice
> Touch worcestershire sauce
> 2 teaspoons fine-chopped fresh chives
> 2 tablespoons cognac or brandy
> Salt
> Freshly ground white pepper

Mix mayonnaise with tomato catsup. Add heavy cream,
creme fraiche, and horseradish and whisk until smooth. Add
remaining ingredients, season with salt and pepper, and mix
well. Refrigerate.

# Sauce Ravigote

*Yields 2½ cups*

*This is a chilled green mayonnaise herb sauce with a strong, crisp, piquant flavor. It is excellent with any cold poached seafood; the Abbey serves it with poached fresh king salmon.*

¾ cup mayonnaise (page 50)
¼ cup creme fraiche (page 49)

1 small bunch Italian parsley
2 tablespoons fresh tarragon leaves
3 tablespoons snipped fresh dill
¼ cup watercress leaves
3 tablespoons chopped fresh chives
½ cup fresh spinach leaves
4 tablespoons capers
1 tablespoon brown seedless mustard
Salt
Freshly ground white pepper
Juice from ½ to 1 lemon
Touch worcestershire sauce

Blanch parsley, tarragon, dill, watercress, chives, and spinach in boiling water for one minute. Drain and then cool in ice water. Squeeze out all water, then place puree with the capers in a food processor or blender. Mix this puree with mayonnaise, creme fraiche, and mustard. Season with salt, pepper, lemon juice, and worcestershire sauce and chill.

# mayonnaise Mustard Oill Sauce

*Yield 1¼ cups*

*This creamy sauce is excellent with cold lobster or other cold seafood appetizers. The flavors of mustard and sugar come through in a definite but still subtle way.*

½ cup mayonnaise (page 50)

2 tablespoons brown sugar
¼ cup heavy cream
2 tablespoons chopped fresh dill
Juice from ½ lemon
Touch worcestershire sauce
1½ tablespoons brown seedless mustard
Salt
Freshly ground white pepper

Moisten brown sugar with a little water and cook for two to three minutes over medium heat. Cool. Mix mayonnaise with heavy cream until smooth. Stir in brown sugar, lemon juice, worcestershire sauce, and mustard. Season with salt and pepper. Chill.

# maitre d'hotel Butter

*Yields 8 ounces*

*This butter is commonly served as a garnish to grilled meats; but I also use it in place of plain butter as the final step in smoothing out a sauce. Dill butter and Colbert butter are variations of maitre d'hotel butter, excellent atop grilled fish.*

> 1 teaspoon glace de viande (page 6), optional
>
> ½ pound salted butter, at room temperature
> Juice from 1-2 lemons
> Touch salt
> Touch freshly ground white pepper
> Pinch Hungarian paprika
> 3 teaspoons fine-chopped parsley
> Dash of worcestershire sauce

Using an electric mixer, blender, or food processor (at lowest speed), or by hand, incorporate all ingredients thoroughly into softened butter.

Place butter near the edge of a piece of wax paper and roll to form a paper-covered cylinder, 1 to 1½ inches in diameter.

Store in refrigerator and slice as needed.

**Fresh Dill Butter.** Prepare as for Maitre d'Hotel Butter, but do not include glace de viande and paprika; instead use two teaspoons fine-chopped fresh dill.

**Colbert Butter.** Prepare as for Maitre d'Hotel Butter, but add 1½ teaspoons chopped fresh tarragon.

## anchovy Butter
*Yields ½ pound*

*Anchovy paste and a touch of worcestershire and lemon make a strongly flavored butter good for use with grilled fish or even grilled steak.*

> ½ pound unsalted butter, at room temperature
> Freshly ground white pepper to taste
> Lemon juice from 1-2 lemons
> Dash of worcestershire sauce
> 1 teaspoon chopped parsley
> Anchovy paste to taste

Using an electric mixer, blender, or food processor (at lowest speed), or by hand, incorporate all ingredients thoroughly into softened butter.

Place butter near the edge of a piece of wax paper and roll to form a paper-covered cylinder, 1½ to 2 inches in diameter.

Store in refrigerator and slice as needed.

# Lobster Butter

*Yields 2 pounds*

*Lobster butter is a highly concentrated butter that has absorbed the flavors of the lobster shells with which it is made. It can easily be frozen and used a little at a time to enhance the flavor of lobster bisque or lobster sauce, or to make a light lobster sauce out of a standard veloute sauce. You can also make crayfish butter the same way, substituting crayfish shells for the lobster shells.*

> 2 pounds salted butter
> 1 dozen lobster shells, cut into pieces
> 1 carrot, diced
> 1 celery stalk, diced
> 1 onion, peeled and diced
> 1 garlic clove, peeled
> Touch cayenne pepper
> Salt to taste
> Freshly ground white pepper to taste

Melt half of the butter in a soup pot; add all the other ingredients. Simmer for 30 to 40 minutes over low to medium heat, stirring frequently. Do not let vegetables brown. Cool slightly, then blend well in a blender or food processor.

Return to pot, add the remaining butter, and simmer for 15 to 20 minutes. Add water to cover all the ingredients. Bring to a boil, remove from the heat, and strain through a fine sieve or cheesecloth. Correct seasoning if necessary. Refrigerate.

After several hours of cooling, the lobster-flavored butter will separate from the water and is very easy to remove. Store in a covered container in the refrigerator.

# Montpellier Butter

*Yields 1½ pounds*

*This is a green herb butter with a sharp, fresh flavor from the anchovies, garlic, capers, and dill pickles. Good for use with fish.*

> 1 cup chopped raw spinach
> ⅓ cup chopped fresh tarragon
> ½ cup chopped fresh parsley
> ½ cup chopped watercress
>
> 1 shallot, chopped
> 4-5 anchovy filets
> 1 garlic clove, peeled
> 1 teaspoon capers
> 1 teaspoon chopped dill pickles
> 1 pound butter, at room temperature
> Salt
> Freshly ground white pepper
> Pinch cayenne pepper
> Juice from ½ to 1 lemon

Blanch the clean, chopped greens for one minute, cool in ice water, and drain well.

Mince blanched greens, shallot, anchovy filets, garlic, capers, and pickles. Add to softened butter with cayenne pepper and lemon juice. Season with salt and pepper and blend thoroughly. Place mixture near the edge of a piece of wax paper and roll to form a paper-covered cylinder 1½ to 2 inches in diameter.

Refrigerate and slice as needed.

# appetizers
# and salads

IN ITS FLAVOR, in its color, and even in the amount of food that it contains, an appetizer should provide a pleasant contrast to the entree that it precedes. When it comes before an elaborate main dish, it can be simple and fresh, requiring little preparation, such as the fine smoked salmon, caviar, and pate de foie gras that can be purchased at a good gourmet store; or it can be complex and exotic, preceding a simple, classic entree. In any case, the small size of the appetizer allows the diner to sample something that might be new to his palate, and to whet his appetite for the dish that is in preparation in the kitchen.

I believe that the decorative presentation of an appetizer does as much to increase its enjoyment as its careful preparation does; and in my kitchen at the Abbey I pay careful attention to the decoration of every plate. Beside some of our shellfish appetizers, for example, we place the shell of a small whole crayfish; but the home chef without access to such decoration can display equal imagination. A slice of lemon, a sprig of parsley or watercress, a small dish of worcestershire sauce on the side can tantalize the eye as the aroma does in its own way. And a salad tossed and garnished at the table can add special enjoyment to its taste for the diner who has watched.

Betweeen the appetizer course and the entree, it provides a special touch to serve a small intermezzo of sherbet, to refresh the palate. Especially if each course is accompanied by a different wine, it is a nice idea to serve a glass of sparkling mineral water along with the intermezzo.

## CReVettes Cocktail kempinski
## Shrimp and Grapefruit Cocktail
*Serves 8*

*We serve this unusual shrimp cocktail in a basket made from a hollowed-out grapefruit. The large shrimp and grapefruit sections are delicious with the creamy pink Marie Louise sauce with its accents of cognac and horseradish. I named the dish after the famous Hotel Kempinski in Berlin.*

2 cups Marie Louise sauce (page 52)

1 carrot
1 stalk celery
1 leek, white part only
2 onions, peeled
Salt
25 black peppercorns, crushed
2 lemons, halved
1 tablespoon pickling spice

40 large headless fresh shrimp

4 grapefruit

2 heads Boston lettuce
Watercress
8 slices lemon
8 slices lime

## To cook shrimp

Wash carrot, celery and leek, and chop these and the onions into large pieces. In a large pot, combine these vegetables with two gallons of salted water and peppercorns, lemon halves, and pickling spice. Bring to a boil, reduce heat, and simmer ten minutes. Add shrimp and bring again to a boil; then simmer five minutes.

Remove shrimp from water, cool, peel, and devein. Refrigerate shrimp and discard cooking liquid.

## To prepare grapefruit

Using a sharp paring knife, cut off both ends of each grapefruit. Resting one cut end on a flat surface, slice off all skin and membrance so that the flesh of the grapefruit is exposed. No white part should remain.

Holding a grapefruit in one hand over a bowl, carefully slice the fruit of each section away from the membranes dividing them. Save the juice that drips into the bowl; it is used in the Marie Louise sauce. Refrigerate the fruit sections and juice. Discard all membranes.

## To serve

Wash lettuce and pat dry, discarding the outer leaves. Arrange the lettuce on individual serving plates. Then, on each plate, form two rows, alternating grapefruit sections and shrimp. Garnish with watercress and lemon and lime slices. Spoon Marie Louise sauce over the grapefruit and shrimp and serve at once.

ARtichaut "pRincesse" au GRatin
## Artichoke filled with Fine Ragout and Asparagus

*Serves 8*

*A highly decorative dish that could easily serve as a light main dish. Prepare the ragout and the artichokes ahead of time, then fill the hollowed-out artichokes and top at the last minute with hollandaise sauce and asparagus tips.*

*To prepare artichokes and asparagus*

> 8 artichokes
> 3-4 lemons
> Salt
> 24 stalks fresh green asparagus
> Sugar

Wash artichokes well. Cut off the top of the artichokes and trim the top of the leaves with scissors. Slice a lemon in half and rub lemon juice on all of the flat cut surfaces.

Add remaining lemon juice to enough salted water to later cover the artichokes. (You may need to use more than one pot.) Bring to a boil; then drop in artichokes. Cover and bring again to a boil; then simmer for 45 minutes, or until artichokes are tender.

Drain artichokes upside down in a colander and cool for 20 minutes.

Spread the leaves open carefully and, using a spoon, remove the inner hairy choke and heart. The artichoke, with its leaves still intact, is ready to be filled. Set aside.

Trim the thick bottoms from the asparagus stalks. Immerse in boiling salted water with a touch of sugar. Cook until done, but still crisp, about 10 minutes. Do not overcook. Plunge immediately into ice water and then drain well. Cut off the top three inches of each stalk; you will use only these tips. (Save the rest of the asparagus for another dish.)

*To prepare meat*

> ½ pound veal sweetbreads
> 2 carrots
> 2 stalks celery
> 2 leeks, white part only
> 2 onions, peeled
> Thyme, 2 sprigs fresh or ¼ teaspoon dried
> Bay leaves, 8-10 fresh or 5-6 dried
> 6-8 whole cloves
> 20-24 black peppercorns
> Salt
> ¾ pound veal (shank or shoulder) meat
> 1 small veal tongue

Wash sweetbreads and soak in cold water for 30 minutes to one hour.

Wash carrots, celery, and leek well; chop these and the onions into large pieces. Place half of the vegetables and half of the herbs and spices into a pot with enough salted water to later cover the veal meat completely. Bring to a boil, reduce heat, and simmer for about 10 minutes. Then add the veal shank or shoulder meat and boil gently for 30 minutes. Then add the soaked sweetbreads to the pot and simmer for about 15 minutes more, or until both meat and sweetbreads are done to your liking.

Using a slotted spoon, remove the meat and sweetbreads and set them aside to cool. Strain the stock; then return it to a low heat. Simmering, uncovered, reduce the stock by one third. Save this reduced stock for use in the sauce.

Place remaining vegetables, herbs, and spices into a pot with enough salted water to later cover the tongue. Bring to a boil; then simmer for 10 minutes. Then add the tongue and boil gently for about 1½ hours. Cool the cooked tongue; then remove the heavy skin around it. Discard this skin and the cooking liquid.

Clean the cooled sweetbreads by removing their skin. Dice the skinned sweetbreads and tongue and the veal meat into ¼-to-½-inch cubes. Set aside.

*To prepare fine ragout*

    1 teaspoon creme fraiche (page 49)

    5 tablespoons butter
    1 onion, peeled and fine chopped
    1½ to 2 tablespoons flour
    ½ cup heavy cream
    ½ cup dry white wine
    1 cup veal stock, saved from previous step
    Dash worcestershire sauce
    Juice from 1 lemon
    ½ cup diced fresh mushrooms
    2-3 egg yolks

Saute mushrooms in one tablespoon of the butter and set aside. Separately, saute the onion in two tablespoons of the butter for three to five minutes, or until translucent but not browned. Add flour to the onions and stir well. Add half of the cream and all of the wine and veal stock. Bring to a boil, stirring constantly. Stir in Worcestershire sauce, lemon juice, and salt and pepper to taste. Simmer for 15 minutes. Sauce should have a fairly heavy, creamy consistency. Whisk in the remaining two tablespoons of butter bit by bit. Stir in creme fraiche and bring to a boil. Strain through a fine sieve.

Return strained sauce to lowest heat and add diced veal, sweetbreads, tongue, and sauteed mushrooms. Bring once again to a boil. Reduce heat to lowest setting.

Mix egg yolks with remaining cream and pour into sauce slowly, stirring constantly with a rubber spatula. To thicken, let sauce barely simmer for about two minutes, still stirring; then remove from heat.

*To serve*

    ½ cup hollandaise sauce (page 48)

    8 teaspoons grated Parmesan cheese
    8 lemon wedges
    Watercress

Heat artichokes and asparagus briefly in lightly salted water; drain. Place artichokes into individual dishes and spoon the fine ragout into each one. Top each with three asparagus tips and drizzle with hollandaise. Sprinkle with Parmesan cheese and broil until cheese is lightly browned.

Garnish with a lemon wedge and watercress. Serve immediately.

## avocat a l'adam
# Avocado Stuffed with Crabmeat
*Serves 8*

*This colorful and delectable dish is a constant favorite at the Abbey. Fresh lump crabmeat is served in an avocado bed with curry cream mayonnaise providing a delightful contrast. If fresh crabmeat is not available, frozen king crab or lobster or shrimp might be substituted by the home cook.*

1 recipe curry cream mayonnaise (page 51)

2 heads Boston lettuce
4 ripe avocados
1½ pounds fresh lump crabmeat
8 strawberries
8 slices cantaloupe
8 small clusters of seedless grapes
16 orange segments, free of membranes
8 slices lime
8 slices lemon
16 slices kiwi fruit
8 sprigs fresh dill

Wash lettuce well and pat dry; arrange the leaves on individual serving plates. Split avocados in half lengthwise, remove pit, and peel. Slice each half into four to five lengthwise pieces and set these closely together in the center of each plate on top of the lettuce leaves, retaining the half avocado shape. Divide the lump crabmeat into eight servings (three ounces each) and place into center of each avocado "half." Surround the avocado with fresh fruit and top crabmeat with curry cream mayonnaise, garnishing with fresh dill.

# Steak Lucullus Garni
## Steak Tartare with Smoked Eel
*Serves 4*

*The rich, smoky taste of the eel contrasts with the fine steak tartare for an unusual variation on this classic dish. Lean top round can be substituted for tenderloin; and the appetizer can be garnished with any number of piquant cold morsels.*

1 pound trimmed beef tenderloin
6-8 anchovy filets
1 tablespoon capers
1 onion, fine chopped
1 teaspoon Hungarian paprika
1-2 garlic cloves, minced
3-4 egg yolks
½ tablespoon salad oil
1 tablespoon chopped parsley
Salt
Freshly ground white pepper
1 tablespoon cognac, optional
Squeeze of lemon juice

1 head Boston lettuce
½ pound fresh smoked eel, skin and bones removed
Capers
Cornichons
Hard-cooked egg
Radish roses
Tomato slices

Butter
White toast or pumpernickel

Trim tenderloin of any fat left by butcher. Chop meat into chunks; then mince very fine with a large French knife or with a meat grinder using a medium-sized blade.

Place anchovy filets and capers in a large bowl. With the back of a fork, mash to a fine paste. Add onion, paprika, and garlic. Mix well; then add egg yolks, oil, and parsley. Mix thoroughly; then blend in meat. Season with salt and pepper. Add cognac if desired and a squeeze of lemon juice. Mix once more.

Divide into four portions. Place on appetizer plates lined with leaves of Boston lettuce. Decorate with slices of smoked eel, capers, cornichons, hard-cooked egg, radish roses, and tomato slices. Serve with fresh butter and white toast or pumpernickel.

## mousselines òe Coquille St. Jacques avec Saumon
## Scallop Mousselines with Smoked Salmon
*Serves 8*

*A very pretty dish that is simpler than it looks in this day of the food processor. The fluffy, airy mousselines are arranged atop thin slices of smoked salmon, with fresh asparagus alongside, and then topped with a hot herbed cream sauce. Norwegian, Irish, and Scottish smoked salmon are all good, but I use Irish salmon at the Abbey. Note: These mousselines can also be prepared with crabmeat or salmon instead of scallops, and are delicious with a wide variety of other dishes.*

*To prepare mousselines (yields 32)*

    1 quart fish stock (page 9)

    ½ pound fresh scallops
    Salt
    Freshly ground white pepper
    Touch of nutmeg
    Pinch of cayenne pepper
    ½ cup heavy cream
    6-8 egg whites

Place scallops with seasonings in a blender or food processor and blend very fine. Turn off machine. Add heavy cream and egg whites and mix with a rubber spatula just until combined. Then process on high speed for 15 to 20 seconds—do not overbeat the cream and egg whites. You should now have a very smooth mixture. Place into a bowl set into a larger bowl filled with ice. Refrigerate for at least one hour.

In a shallow pan, bring fish stock to a gentle boil; then reduce to a simmer. Dip a teaspoon into the simmering stock. Using this warmed teaspoon, dip a small amount of cooled mousseline (the size and shape of an unshelled walnut) and gently slide it into the stock. Repeat this until you have 32 mousselines. Simmer for five minutes; then keep warm in the stock. Remove a half cup of the fish stock and save for the sauce.

*To prepare sauce*

    2½ tablespoons butter
    2 tablespoons fine-chopped shallots
    1 tablespoon flour
    ½ cup heavy cream
    ½ cup fish stock, saved in previous step
    ¼ cup dry white wine
    Salt
    Freshly ground white pepper
    Juice of ½ lemon
    1 teaspoon fine-chopped fresh chives
    1 teaspoon fine-chopped fresh Italian parsley
    1 teaspoon fine-chopped fresh dill
    2 egg yolks

Melt 1½ tablespoons butter in a pot. Saute shallots for three to four minutes, until translucent but not browned. Add flour and stir well. Add two-thirds of the heavy cream and bring to a boil. Stir in fish stock and white wine; then reduce heat.

Sprinkle with salt and pepper and add lemon juice. Simmer for about 10 minutes. Whisk in the remaining butter bit by bit. Add creme fraiche and simmer for five minutes, stirring constantly. Strain through a fine sieve or cheesecloth; then return to heat. Add chives, parsley, and dill while barely simmering. Beat the egg yolks with the remaining cream. Then slowly whisk this into the sauce. Stirring constantly, warm for about two more minutes, but do not let sauce boil or hardly simmer any more. Remove from heat. Heat asparagus briefly in lightly salted water.

*To serve*

> 16 thin slices smoked salmon
> 32 4-inch tips cooked green asparagus

Lay two slices of smoked salmon side by side on individual dishes. Arrange four scallop mousselines diagonally across the salmon. Place two pieces of warm asparagus on each side of the mousselines. Spoon hot sauce over mousselines and serve immediately.

**Crabmeat or salmon mousselines.** Prepare as for scallop mousselines, but substitute the same weight of fresh crabmeat or salmon for the scallops. These can be prepared without the sauce above to accompany a variety of dishes.

## Terrine de Canard Pistache Madame Prissy
# Duck Terrine with Pistachios
*Serves 10 to 12*

*Created on a special occasion for Prissy Swearingen, wife of the Abbey's owner, this lovely cold appetizer blends the subtle flavors of pistachio and cognac with green peppercorns and fresh ginger. Do not use a food processor to grind the duck meat; the mixture should be coarse, with small bits of meat within it. It is served at the Abbey decorated with Madeira aspic and garnished with tomato roses, radishes, and slices of hard-cooked egg.*

¾ pound pork (Boston butt)
¾ pound veal (shoulder)
½ pound deboned fresh duck leg meat, skin removed
¼ pound pork fat
½ pound duck liver
½ pound duck breast
¾ pound roasted duck
Salt
Freshly ground white pepper
Coarsely ground fresh black pepper
1½ green peppercorns (brine-packed)
3-4 dried bay leaves
¾ teaspoon dried thyme
Freshly ground nutmeg (or mace)
¼ teaspoon ground cloves
½ teaspoon coriander
½ teaspoon ground cinnamon
½ teaspoon fine-chopped fresh ginger
3 tablespoons shelled, chopped pistachio nuts
3-4 tablespoons cognac
6 thin slices fatback, approximately 6 inches square

Chop the pork, veal, and duck leg into chunks.

In a large pot, bring a half gallon of salted water to a boil. Place the first four ingredients into the boiling water and blanch for one to two minutes. Remove meat from water with a slotted spoon. While still warm, transfer this meat to a meat grinder fitted with a large blade. The mixture should still contain small bits of meat after grinding.

Dice the duck liver and breast into 1/8-inch pieces and the roasted duck into quarter-inch pieces. In a large bowl, combine this diced meat with the ground meat and mix by hand. Blend in all spices, nuts, and cognac thoroughly.

Line one large or two small terrine molds with fatback so that bottom and sides are completely covered. Pack the meat mixture firmly into the molds, about ¾ full. Cover the mixture with slices of fatback.

Place terrines into a deep baking pan filled with water, so that at least half of the sides of the terrine mold are covered with water. Bake in a preheated 300-325°F oven for approximately 1½ hours.

Remove molds from baking pan and allow to cool to room temperature. Refrigerate for several hours or overnight.

Loosen edges of terrine by running a sharp knife around the sides of the mold, and unmold.

Serve two quarter-inch thick slices of terrine per person on a plate lined with lettuce and garnished as desired.

# Saumon Marine a l'abbe
## Marinated King Salmon with Mustard Dill Sauce
*Serves 15 to 20*

*This Scandinavian delicacy is served with a wonderful sweet and spicy mustard sauce and dark bread. I have found that salmon will hold its firm texture and reddish color better if the whole salmon is frozen before fileting and marinating; the touch of saltpeter in the marinade also helps keep the color just right. Plan ahead for this dish; the salmon must marinate for several days.*

> 1 filet of king salmon (approximately 3-4 pounds), trimmed, bottom skin left on
> 4 tablespoons salt
> 9 tablespoons sugar
> Pinch saltpeter, optional
> Freshly ground black pepper
> 1 tablespoon crushed juniper berries
> 1 lemon
> 2 onions, peeled and chopped fine
> 5 bunches fresh dill with stems (or 5-6 tablespoons dried dill weed)
> 3 cups salad oil
>
> Sliced hard-cooked egg
> Radish roses
> Tomato roses or slices
> Fine-chopped onions
> Dark bread

Remove bones protruding from salmon. (Pliers may be useful for this.) Lay salmon in a large shallow pan or dish.

Mix salt, sugar, and saltpeter (optional) and rub into the salmon filet on the skinless side only. Sprinkle the pepper and juniper berries on the salmon. Spread the entire salmon with the chopped onions and place fresh dill on top. Pour oil carefully over salmon, so as not to disturb the toppings. Cover the entire fish with cheesecloth and weight it down. (A cutting board is good for this purpose.) Marinate for approximately three days.

Remove salmon from marinade; scrape excess oil, dill, and onions from the fish; and place it on a cutting board. Beginning at the tail end, slice salmon very thin, on the diagonal.

Arrange slices on serving plates. Decorate with sliced boiled egg, radish roses, tomato roses or slices and fine-chopped onions. Serve with sweet mustard dill sauce on the side (recipe follows) and dark bread.

*To prepare sauce*

   ¾ cup water
   ¾ cup brown sugar
   1 cup prepared brown seedless mustard
   ⅓ cup chopped fresh dill

Bring water to a boil, add sugar, and boil for approximately 10 minutes, stirring occasionally with a wire whip. When mixture is syrupy and smooth, add mustard and simmer for five to eight more minutes, stirring frequently. Allow to cool and mix in fresh chopped dill. Refrigerate until cold before serving.

# homard de Maine Parisienne
# Cold Maine Lobster with Vegetable Salad

*Serves 8*

*An elegant dish for a summer party, using a variety of fresh garden vegetables. The lobster is cooked and removed from the split shells, which are then filled with chilled vegetable salad and lobster medallions, garnished with caviar, and served with a mayonnaise mustard dill sauce.*

*To prepare lobster*

> 1 carrot
> 1 celery stalk
> 1 leek, white part only
> 2 onions, peeled
> Salt
> 25 crushed black peppercorns
> 2 lemons, halved
> 4 Maine lobsters, 1¼-1½ pounds each

Wash carrot, celery, and leek; chop these and the onions into large pieces. Place all ingredients except lobster into two gallons of boiling, salted water. Boil for 10 to 15 minutes. Add lobsters, cover, bring to boil again and then simmer for 12 to 15 minutes. Remove lobsters from water and allow to cool. Discard water and vegetables.

To remove meat from lobsters, first pull off claws and legs; then lay lobsters on their backs. Using scissors, trim away the soft part of the shell on the lobster's tail, being careful not to separate tail from body. Remove tail meat. Split lobster shell lengthwise from head to tail with a sharp knife. Clean out shells completely, rinsing under cold water, and save them to be filled with the vegetable salad.

Slice each tail into eight medallions and remove veins. Crack claws with lobster or nut cracker. Pull out meat intact if possible. Also remove and save any extra bits of lobster meat. Refrigerate until ready to use.

*To prepare vegetable salad*

> ½ cup mayonnaise (see recipe, page 50)
>
> 1 pound fresh, crisp, cooked vegetables such as carrots, green beans, cauliflower, mushrooms, peas, broccoli, asparagus, etc.
> Extra bits of meat from lobster
> Salt
> Freshly ground white pepper
> Touch worcestershire sauce
> Juice of ½ lemon
> 2 tablespoons chopped fresh parsley

Dice cooked vegetables into half-inch cubes.

Fold vegetables and lobster meat gently into mayonnaise so vegetables are not crushed. Add seasonings, lemon, and parsley. Refrigerate until ready to use.

*To serve*

> 1 recipe mayonnaise mustard dill sauce (page 54)
>
> 2 heads Boston, bibb, or other soft lettuce
> Bunch fresh parsley, washed
> 1 tomato
> 1 lemon
> 2 hard-cooked eggs
> 8 teaspoons good black caviar, optional

Wash lettuce leaves and pat dry. Arrange on individual oblong serving plates. Set a half lobster shell in the center of each plate. Completely fill tail portion of each shell with vegetable salad. Place one claw on top of salad and layer four medallions of lobster to fill the body section. Fill empty head portion of shell with parsley. Garnish the plate with slices of tomato, lemon, and egg. Top each lobster medallion with ¼ teaspoon caviar, if desired. Serve mayonnaise mustard dill sauce separately.

## Saumon Poche Froid, Sauce Ravigote
## Chilled Poached Salmon

*Serves 8 to 10*

*This delicate cold appetizer is served with a chilled green mayonnaise herb sauce. Both the salmon and the sauce can be prepared well ahead of time. At the Abbey we garnish the salmon with aspic and decorate the plate with lemon and cucumber "flowers."*

*To prepare fish*

> 3 quarts fish stock (page 9)
>
> 1 recipe ravigote sauce (page 53)
>
> 6 tablespoons butter
> 2-3 shallots, chopped fine
> 2 cups dry white wine
> Juice from 2-3 lemons
> 1 whole side of fresh king salmon; boned, trimmed, skin intact

Melt butter in a long shallow pan. Add shallots and saute for three to four minutes. Then add fish stock, white wine, and lemon juice. Bring to a boil, lay side of salmon into pan (salmon should be covered with stock); then simmer about 15 minutes or until salmon is done. Carefully remove from pan, allow to cool, and then refrigerate for several hours.

*To serve*

    2 heads Boston lettuce
    2 ripe tomatoes
    2 hard-cooked eggs
    8 lemon wedges or slices
    8 slices of lime
    8 radishes
    Watercress

Wash lettuce well and gently pat dry. Remove skin from poached salmon and discard. Divide lettuce leaves among individual serving plates. Slice salmon into eight portions and place one on each plate. Decorate with the tomatoes, egg, lemon, lime, radishes, and watercress. Spoon chilled ravigote sauce over salmon and serve.

# Gratinee du Crab Louisienne "Dante"
# Louisiana Crabmeat "Dante"

*Serves 8*

*Large mushroom caps are filled with a creamy spiced crabmeat mixture, topped with hollandaise sauce and Parmesan cheese, and served hot.*

*To prepare crabmeat stuffing*

   ¼ cup fish stock (page 9)
   1 tablespoon creme fraiche (page 49)

   5 tablespoons butter
   1 shallot, chopped fine
   2-3 green onions, chopped fine
   ½ cup diced mushrooms
   1 tablespoon flour
   ½ cup heavy cream
   ½ cup dry white wine
   Bay leaves, 2-3 fresh or 1-2 dried
   Salt
   Freshly ground white pepper
   1 clove garlic, minced
   Touch of worcestershire sauce
   Touch of Tabasco
   Juice from 1½ lemons
   1½ pounds fresh lump crabmeat, shelled
   2 tomatoes

Peel tomatoes. Remove seeds, dice, and saute in a tablespoon of the butter; set aside.

Melt two tablespoons of the butter in a pot over medium heat. Add shallots, green onions, and mushrooms; saute for three to four minutes. Remove from heat, add flour, and stir well. Add heavy cream, fish stock, and two-thirds of the white wine. Return to heat and, stirring well, add bay leaves, a sprinkling of salt and pepper, garlic, worcestershire sauce, Tabasco, and juice from one lemon. Bring to a boil; then simmer for about 15 minutes, stirring frequently. Add creme fraiche and blend well. Using a rubber spatula, carefully fold in the fresh lump crabmeat so that the crabmeat does not fall apart. Add sauteed tomatoes. Bring to a boil again and cook for about two minutes more. Correct seasonings and set aside.

*To prepare mushrooms and serve*

> ½ cup hollandaise sauce (page 48)
> 32 firm, white mushroom caps
> ½ cup grated Parmesan cheese
> Parsley
> 8 lemon wedges

Wash mushrooms well and remove stems. Saute mushroom caps in the remaining butter until lightly browned. (The mushrooms should lie flat on the bottom of a skillet as you do this.) Season with salt and pepper, the juice from half a lemon, and the remaining white wine. Simmer until mushrooms are done, but still firm.

Place four mushroom caps on each individual serving dish. Fill each cap with the crabmeat stuffing and drizzle with hollandaise sauce. Sprinkle with Parmesan cheese and broil until cheese is lightly browned.

Garnish with parsley and lemon and serve immediately.

# Escargots aux fines herbes
## Snails in White Wine Herb Sauce

*Serves 8*

*At the Abbey we use French Burgundy snails, which are the finest to be had, in this delicate herbed preparation.*

*To prepare snails*

> 2 tablespoons butter
> ¼ cup fine-chopped shallots
> 4-5 green onions, chopped fine
> 48 medium to large snails
> 2 garlic cloves, minced
> Salt
> Freshly ground white pepper
> ¼ cup dry white wine
> Juice from ½ lemon

Rinse snails thoroughly under cold water.

Heat butter in a skillet and saute shallots and green onions for three to four minutes, but do not brown. Add snails, garlic, a sprinkling of salt and pepper, white wine, and lemon juice. Cook for four or five minutes, remove from heat, and set aside.

*To prepare sauce*

> ½ cup fish stock (page 9)
> 2 tablespoons creme fraiche (page 49)
>
> 2½ tablespoons butter
> 2 tablespoons fine-chopped shallots
> 1 tablespoon flour
> ½ cup heavy cream
> ¼ cup dry white wine
> Salt

Freshly ground white pepper
Juice of ½ lemon
1 teaspoon fine-chopped fresh chives
1 teaspoon chopped parsley
8-12 leaves of watercress
1 tablespoon chopped fresh sorrel
Parmesan cheese, grated
Watercress for garnish
8 lemon wedges

Melt 1½ tablespoons of the butter in a medium saucepan. Saute shallots for three to four minutes, until translucent but not browned. Add flour and stir well. Add heavy cream and bring to a boil. Blend in fish stock and white wine. Stirring frequently, boil again and then simmer until reduced by a third. Sprinkle with salt, pepper, and lemon juice. Whisk in the remaining butter bit by bit. Stirring constantly, add cream fraiche and simmer for five more minutes. Strain through a fine sieve or cheesecloth. Return to heat. Add chives, parsley, watercress, and sorrel and bring once again to a boil; then simmer for three or four minutes. Add snails to the sauce and heat for a few moments. Adjust seasonings if necessary.

Place six snails into each individual serving dish. Cover with sauce, sprinkle with Parmesan cheese, and brown slightly under a broiler. Garnish with watercress and lemon wedges.

# Moules Gratinées aux Épinards
# Fresh Mussels Baked with Spinach

*Serves 8*

*Seasoned cooked spinach is topped with fresh mussels and a creamy sauce and served hot. Be sure to have a few extra mussels on hand in case some prove to be bad. The clean empty mussel shells make a lovely decoration on the serving plate.*

*To prepare mussels and spinach*

>    4 tablespoons butter
>    1 large onion, peeled and chopped fine
>    Salt
>    Pinch saffron threads
>    Freshly ground black pepper
>    Juice of 1 lemon
>    1 cup dry white wine
>    1 bunch parsley, washed
>    3 garlic cloves, minced
>    Bay leaves, 4-5 fresh or 2-3 dried
>    Mussels to serve 6-8 per person
>    2-2½ pounds fresh spinach (yields ⅓ to ½ cup servings)

Scrub mussels well and rinse thoroughly in cold water.

In a large pot, saute onion in butter until translucent. Add two cups of salted water and all the other ingredients except mussels. Bring to a boil; then simmer for several minutes. Add mussels, stir well, cover, and simmer three to five minutes, until mussels open. Remove mussels from stock and discard any unopened ones. Set aside good mussels to cool. Carefully strain stock through a fine sieve or cheesecloth. (Any sand left on the bottom of the pot should be kept out of the stock when straining.) Reserve stock for sauce.

When mussels are cool enough to handle, take them out of the shell and remove their black rims.

(recipe continues on page 85)

*Photographs on the following pages portray these recipes:*

Plate I.
Cold Hors d'Oeuvres (from front, clockwise)
   *Homard de Maine Parisienne*
   Cold Maine Lobster with Vegetable Salad *(page 75)*

   *Saumon Marine a l'Abbe*
   Marinated Salmon with Sweet Mustard Dill Sauce *(page 73)*

   *Terrine de Canard Pistache Madame Prissy*
   Duck Terrine with Pistachios *(page 71)*

   *Salade des Epinards Nouvelle Epoque*
   Fresh Spinach Salad with Duck Liver *(page 89)*

   *Avocat a l'Adam*
   Avocado Stuffed with Crabmeat *(page 66)*

Plate II.
*Bouillabaisse Marseillaise*
Fisherman's Stew *(page 98)*

Plate III.
*Filet de Truite Farci a l'Abbe*
Trout Filled with Salmon Mousse *(page 108)*

Plate IV.
*Oie Rotie a la Suedoise*
Swedish Roast Goose *(page 123)*

Plate V.
*Escalope de Veau Nouvelle Bertram*
Veal Cutlet Filled with Mushrooms and Herbs *(page 148)*

Plate VI.
*Selle d'Agneau en Feuilletage*
Saddle of Lamb in Puff Pastry *(page 158)*

Plate VII.
*Medaillons de Porc Milanaise*
Pork Medallions Milanaise *(page 161)*

Plate VIII.
Assorted Desserts

Blanch washed spinach in boiling water; then chill quickly in ice water. Drain well and pat off excess water.

*To prepare sauce and serve*

2 tablespoons creme fraiche (page 49)

5 tablespoons butter
3 shallots, chopped fine
¼ cup fine-chopped carrots
¼ cup fine-chopped leeks, white part only
¼ cup fine-chopped celery
1 to 1½ tablespoons flour
½ cup heavy cream
¾ cup mussel stock, saved
¼ cup dry white wine
2 garlic cloves, chopped
Bay leaves, 2 fresh or 1 dried
Juice of 1 lemon
Pinch saffron threads
Salt
Freshly ground white pepper
2-3 egg yolks
Freshly ground or grated nutmeg
8 tablespoons grated Gruyere or Swiss cheese

Melt two tablespoons of the butter in a large saucepan over medium heat. Add half of the shallots and all of the chopped vegetables. Saute for three to five minutes. Add flour and mix well. Add half of the cream and all the mussel stock and white wine. Bring to a boil, stirring occasionally. Add garlic, bay leaves, lemon juice, and saffron threads. Season with salt and pepper. Simmer for about 15 minutes. Whisk two tablespoons of the butter into the sauce bit by bit; then add creme fraiche, mix well, and continue to simmer.

Beat the remaining cream and the egg yolks together. Slowly pour into the sauce, stirring constantly. Continue to stir over lowest heat for about two more minutes, but do not let boil or even simmer. Adjust seasonings if necessary and remove from heat.

Melt the remaining tablespoon of butter in a skillet and lightly saute the remaining chopped shallots. Add spinach and season with salt, pepper, and nutmeg. Mix well; then divide onto individual serving plates. Top each with six to eight mussels and ladle a good amount of sauce over these. Top with grated cheese and broil until brown.

## SORBET AU PORTO
## Port Wine Sherbet
*Serves 12*

*This distinctive sherbet can be served either as a dessert or as a refreshing intermezzo between the appetizer and the main course. If you prefer, you can prepare it in the freezer without using an ice cream maker.*

  1 quart water
  1 cup sugar
  Grated peel from ½ lemon
  ½ teaspoon vanilla
  2 cups Port

Bring water and sugar to a boil in a kettle. Add lemon peel and vanilla and bring again to a boil. Remove from heat and cool completely. Then stir in the port.

Prepare your ice cream maker. Pour in the liquid and let it work until it freezes. Store in the freezer.

Alternatively, this sorbet can be made without an ice cream maker. Pour the cooled liquid into a shallow dish or pan and freeze just until slushy, about 2½ to 3 hours. Remove from freezer and beat thoroughly with a fork, whisk, or electric mixer. Return to freezer until hard enough to serve.

Endiues a la Neufchatel
# Endives and Tomatoes with Neufchatel Dip
*Serves 6*

*Belgian endive leaves have a fresh, slightly bitter taste; they
make an excellent light salad, accompanied by this spicy
cream cheese dip.*

½ pound cream cheese, softened
4 tablespoons mayonnaise
4 tablespoons sour cream or creme fraiche (page 49)
2 teaspoons paprika
2 teaspoons curry powder
Touch chopped parsley
Chopped fresh dill
4 scallions, diced fine
1 shallot, chopped fine
Salt
Freshly ground white pepper

1 head romaine lettuce
6 large Belgian endives
3 tomatoes, sliced
Hard-cooked egg, in slices or wedges

Using a blender, food processor, or electric mixer, add mayonnaise, sour cream, paprika, and curry powder to cream cheese
and blend well. Add parsley, dill, scallions, and shallot;
season with salt and pepper. Mix until dip is smooth. If dip is
too thick, add a little fresh cream to it.

On plates lined with romaine leaves, lay endive leaves in a star
pattern. Place slices of tomato in the center and top with the
dip. Garnish with parsley and eggs.

## Salade Maison
# Crabmeat and Vegetable Salad
*Serves 4 to 6*

*Pate de foie gras provides the crowning touch to this rich salad of crabmeat, asparagus, green beans, and carrot.*

*To prepare dressing*

> 3 egg yolks
> ¾ to 1 cup olive oil
> 1 tablespoon prepared mustard
> 2 tablespoons red wine vinegar
> Touch worcestershire sauce
> Touch Hungarian paprika
> Juice from ½ lemon
> Freshly ground white pepper
> Salt
> ½ cup heavy cream

Whisk half of the olive oil into the egg yolks in a slow but steady stream. Stir in mustard, vinegar, worcestershire sauce, paprika, lemon juice, pepper, and salt. Then, still whisking, slowly add the rest of the oil. In a separate bowl, whip heavy cream until it holds soft peaks. Fold cream into dressing.

*To prepare salad*

> 1 cup cooked green beans, chilled
> 1 carrot, julienned
> 8 spears cooked green asparagus, chilled
> 8-10 ounces cooked king crab leg meat, sliced
> 1 cup thin-sliced mushrooms
> 2 heads Boston lettuce, well washed
> 6 ounces pate de foie gras, diced

Slice the asparagus spears in half lengthwise.

Mix beans, carrots, asparagus, half of the crabmeat, and mushrooms. Add dressing and toss slightly.

Arrange lettuce leaves on individual plates and place salad on the lettuce. Top with pate de foie gras and garnish with the remaining crabmeat slices.

## Salaðe ðes Epinarðs nouvelle Epoque
## Fresh Spinach Salad with Duck Liver
*Serves 4 to 6*

*At the Abbey this fresh spinach salad is prepared right at the table. The hot bacon bits are sprinkled over the dressed spinach, a duck liver is sauteed and placed atop the leaves, and the whole is finished off with a flourish of pepper.*

*To prepare dressing*

    4 egg yolks
    4-6 hard-cooked egg yolks
    1 cup olive oil
    Salt
    Freshly ground black pepper
    1-2 garlic cloves, minced
    Juice from ½ lemon
    1 to 1½ tablespoons prepared mustard
    Worcestershire sauce
    Touch of tabasco
    2-3 tablespoons red wine vinegar
    1 tablespoon chopped parsley

In a deep bowl, blend together the raw and cooked egg yolks. Whisk in half of the olive oil in a slow but steady stream. Stir in garlic, lemon juice, mustard, worcestershire sauce, tabasco, and red wine vinegar; season with salt and pepper.

Then whisk in the remaining oil. If dressing is too thick, add a touch of heavy cream to thin slightly. Adjust seasonings if necessary and mix in chopped parsley.

*To prepare salad*

8-10 slices raw bacon
1 pound fresh young spinach
1-2 hard-cooked eggs, chopped fine
1 cup thin-sliced fresh mushrooms
2 tomatoes, sliced
1-2 tablespoons butter
8-10 duck livers
Salt
Freshly ground black pepper

Chop bacon very fine; fry until crisp. Keep hot.

Wash spinach well and pat dry; remove stems. Toss spinach with dressing and transfer onto individual serving dishes. Sprinkle with chopped eggs and sliced mushrooms; garnish with tomato slices.

Clean duck livers and slice one-inch thick; season with salt and pepper. In a skillet, melt butter and saute duck liver over high heat for three to four minutes.

Spoon two tablespoons hot bacon bits over each salad. Top with two to three slices hot duck liver. Sprinkle with freshly ground black pepper.

Salaðe a l'abbe
# Lobster, Chicken, and Ham Salad
*Serves 6*

*This is my version of a Salade Bretonne, created by the great chef Alain Chapel. Red wine vinegar can be substituted for the sherry vinegar if you wish.*

1 1½-pound Maine lobster, boiled and sliced (page 75)

2 boneless breasts of chicken
1 tablespoon butter
6 ounces julienne of cooked ham
2 tablespoons capers
3-4 cornichons or small pickles, julienned
½ cup dry white wine
1 shallot, chopped fine
¼ cup sherry vinegar
1 tablespoon brown seedless mustard
1 clove garlic, minced
½ teaspoon chopped fresh tarragon
½ teaspoon minced fresh chervil
½ teaspoon snipped fresh chives
Juice from ½ lemon
Salt
Freshly ground pepper
¾ cup olive oil
1 head romaine
½ head endive
½ head escarole
1 cup thin-sliced mushrooms
1 tablespoon chopped fresh chives

Lightly saute chicken breasts in butter; add a touch of water and simmer just until tender. Remove from pan, cool, and slice into julienne strips.

Marinate chicken, ham, capers, and cornichons in white wine for 30 minutes, then drain.

In a bowl, combine shallot with vinegar, mustard, garlic, tarragon, chervil, chives, and lemon juice; season with salt and pepper. Add olive oil slowly in a steady stream, whisking until thoroughly blended.

Wash lettuces, discarding outer leaves; gently pat dry. Tear into large pieces and place in a salad bowl. Add drained, marinated chicken mixture and lobster slices. Toss lightly with the herb dressing.

Divide salad among individual plates, sprinkle with sliced mushrooms and chives, and serve.

## Salaðe ðe moules au Safran
# Mussel Salad with Saffron

*Serves 4*

*Long popular in Europe, mussels have only recently enjoyed a vogue in the United States. In some coastal areas they are available free for the picking during the season. Here is a fine cold mussel salad one can easily prepare.*

*To prepare mussels*

> ½ cup fish stock (page 9)
>
> 1 chopped shallot
> 2-3 tablespoons butter
> ¼ cup dry white wine
> Juice from one lemon
> Pinch of saffron
> 1 garlic clove, minced
> Salt
> Freshly ground black pepper
> 1½ pounds fresh mussels, well scrubbed and rinsed

Saute shallots in butter for three minutes. Add fish stock, wine, lemon juice, saffron, and garlic; season with salt and pepper. Bring to a boil; then simmer for five minutes. Add mussels and simmer until mussels are opened. Remove mussels from stock, *discarding any unopened mussels*. Set good mussels aside to cool. Strain stock and cool.

*To prepare dressing*

> 4 egg yolks
> ¾ cup olive oil
> 1 shallot, peeled and diced fine
> 1 teaspoon chopped blanched fresh tarragon
> 1 teaspoon prepared mustard

1 garlic clove, minced
2 tablespoons red wine vinegar
Salt
Freshly ground white pepper

Whisk half of the olive oil into the egg yolks, in a slow but steady stream. Add shallots, tarragon, mustard, garlic, and vinegar; season with salt and pepper. Then slowly whisk in the remaining oil so that you have a fairly thick dressing. Slowly stir in enough of the cooled mussel stock to achieve a creamy, not-too-thick dressing.

*To serve*

4 heads Boston lettuce
Cooked mussels
1 stalk julienne of celery
1-2 tomatoes, peeled and diced
1 tablespoon chopped chives

Wash lettuce, discarding outer leaves, and gently pat dry. Arrange on individual plates. Remove all but eight mussels from shell and trim the black rim from around them. Arrange mussels without shell on top of lettuce, then spoon a little dressing over each mussel. Garnish the salad with the julienne of celery, diced tomatoes, and chopped chives. Decorate each plate with two mussels in the shell.

## Salaðe ðe Concombres et Aneth
# Cucumber Salad with Fresh Dill

*Serves 4 to 6*

*At the Abbey, I serve this salad with grilled fresh salmon and dill butter, or with filet of fresh salmon poached and served with dill sauce.*

> 2 cucumbers, peeled
> Salt
> 4-5 tablespoons red wine vinegar
> Freshly ground white pepper
> 2-3 tablespoons chopped fresh dill
> 4 tablespoons salad oil
> ¾ teaspoon sugar
> 1 to 1½ onions, chopped fine
> 1 tablespoon fresh chopped parsley
> 2-3 tablespoons sour cream

Slice cucumbers very thin; place into a bowl and sprinkle with salt. Cover and refrigerate for one to two hours.

Drain water from cucumbers. Add vinegar, pepper, fresh dill, oil, sugar, onions, and parsley; mix well. Stir in sour cream and season with more salt if needed. Refrigerate for an hour more, then serve.

# fish
# and shellfish

O PREPARE A FISH RECIPE that conforms to the standards of the Abbey, one must begin with the freshest fish to be had, and cook it just to the right degree. It is a difficult operation to cook fish well, requiring experience, patience, and unerring timing; and it can be one of the true tests of the gourmet chef to achieve.

By far my favorite fish, and one that I go to great lengths to obtain at the Abbey, is the delicate, flavorful Dover sole. A flat fish of about six pounds, it is found only in the waters of the North Sea, in the English Channel between Dover, France, and Holland. Its flesh is flaky and snowy white; its taste is incomparable. I have presented my recipe here for preparing it, though in America it will probably be necessary to substitute a native fresh sole instead. As well as the Dover sole, we import the European turbot to the Abbey; and we obtain fresh red snapper from the Gulf of Mexico, sea bass, pompano, scallops, shellfish, Maine lobster, shrimp, and live trout.

I like smaller fish and filets to be sauteed in butter, with the barest trace of flour coating to provide a delicate crust; but especially for a larger fish, poaching in a well-seasoned stock will result in a more delicate and interesting dish. For a large fish, be sure the poaching liquid is cold at the start; this allows the fish to cook more slowly and evenly, and prevents it from splitting open at the shock of the boiling liquid. Smaller fish, of course, should be started in boiling stock, and simmered slowly until done. One of my favorite ways of cooking fish is "fish blue," a traditional European method that can only be achieved with live trout or carp. The natural coating on the skin of the fish, which is killed and cleaned only moments before it is cooked, turns a lovely sky blue when the fish is lowered into the boiling liquid.

Whether it is sauteed, poached, baked, grilled, or broiled, however, the good cook must learn from experience just when the fish is firm, flaky, and perfectly done. Every recipe that I present here is cooked to order only moments before it arrives at the customer's table in the Abbey; and the home chef should take equal care to prepare the ingredients ahead of time, so that the final preparation of the fish in its sauce can be accomplished with speed and ease.

## Bouillabaisse Marseillaise
# Fisherman's Stew

*Serves 6 to 8*

*The traditional Marseilles bouillabaisse is made with fish that are found only in the Mediterranean Sea. Abbey bouillabaisse, flavored strongly with saffron, garlic, and fennel, substitutes the fresh fish available to us: red snapper, sea bass, shrimp, salmon, sole, mussels, clams, and Maine lobster. The base of the soup can be made ahead of time, and the fish added at the last minute so that it will not be overcooked.*

2 cups fish stock (page 9)
1 cup chicken stock (page 8)

¼ cup each diced celery, carrots, onions, and white part of leek
¼ cup olive oil
1 tablespoon butter
3 scallions, chopped
½ cup diced peeled tomatoes
¼ cup tomato paste
½ cup dry white wine
1 teaspoon green peppercorns, in brine
4 cloves garlic, minced
Saffron
2 teaspoons chopped fresh parsley
1 sprig of thyme
Bay leaves, 4-5 fresh or 3 dried
½ teaspoon fennel
Touch of absinthe or anisette or pernod
Salt
Freshly ground white pepper
Approximately 4 pounds assorted fish: snapper, sole, turbot, lobster tails (in shell), scampi, crayfish (in shell), oysters, sea bass, scallops, clams, mullet, etc., cut into 1½-ounce pieces

16 slices French bread, buttered, sprinkled with fresh-minced or powdered garlic and toasted

Saute celery, carrots, onions, and leek in half of the olive oil and the tablespoon of butter for five to eight minutes over medium heat. Add scallions and tomatoes, then tomato paste. Braise for three to four minutes while stirring. Add fish stock, beef or chicken stock, and white wine. Blend in green peppercorns, garlic, saffron, herbs, and absinthe; season with salt and pepper. Simmer for 10 to 15 minutes.

While soup is simmering, pour the remaining olive oil into a large skillet and saute all the fish except for oysters, mussels, and clams for a few minutes. Place all the sauteed fish into the fish soup. Add oysters, clams and mussels and simmer for three to four minutes.

Divide all seafood into individual serving dishes. Pour soup over the fish, sprinkle with chopped parsley, and top each with two garlic croutons.

*Suggested Wines*

Chateau St. Jean Fume Blanc
Mondavi Fume Blanc

## nasi Goreng
## Indonesian Rice Dish
*Serves 4*

*I learned this spicy Indonesian dish when I worked as a chef on a Dutch ship sailing the Atlantic. It is a colorful combination of rice and fresh vegetables, mixed with succulent lobster, shrimp, and veal. The Indonesian spices, imported from Holland, are sometimes available in Oriental grocery stores or gourmet stores. Note: This dish can also be made with noodles instead of rice; it is then called Bami Goreng.*

¾ pound trimmed veal loin
½ cup soy sauce
2 garlic cloves, minced
¼ cup diced carrots, ¼ inch square
¼ cup diced onions, ¼ inch square
¼ cup diced celery, ¼ inch square
¼ cup diced leek, white part only
¼ cup chopped green onion
9 tablespoons butter
6 cups cooked rice
16-20 pearl onions
Salt
Freshly ground white pepper
Indonesian spices:
   Sambal Oelek
   Sambal Badjak
   Sambal Nasi Goreng
   Sambal Udang
   Sambal Trassie
   Sambal Petis
4 3 to 4 ounce lobster tails, shells removed, diced
8-10 large scampi; peeled, deveined, and diced

4 pieces kroepeck (shrimp bread), optional
4 quartered dill pickles

Slice veal into 1½-inch strips. Marinate in soy sauce with garlic for two hours.

In a large skillet, saute carrots, onions, celery, leek, and green onions in three tablespoons of the butter for eight to ten minutes, but do not brown. Add cooked rice and pearl onions, mix well, and place in a 400°F oven until hot, four to five minutes (or on stovetop, stirring constantly). Season with salt and pepper. Then add approximately ¼ teaspoon of each Sambal and mix well into rice. (Be very careful with the very hot Sambal Oelek.) Keep rice warm.

Remove veal from marinade and dry well. Season with salt and pepper.

Heat three tablespoons of the butter in a large skillet. In one of the skillets, over very high heat, sear veal strips quickly, but do not overcook. With a slotted spoon, remove meat from skillet and add to rice.

Season lobster and shrimp meat with salt and pepper and saute separately in the remaining butter. Again, do not over-cook. Add to rice and mix thoroughly.

Fry kroepeck (in oil to cover) for one or two minutes, until it increases to about three times the original size.

Heat pickle quarters in a little water.

Divide rice among serving dishes. Garnish each plate with a quartered pickle and a piece of kroepeck. Serve immediately.

*Suggested Wines*

Joseph Phelps Gewurztraminer
Rutherford Hill Gewurztraminer

Scampi a l'Oseille
## Scampi in Sorrel Sauce
*Serves 4*

*The white sauce with fresh sorrel cut into fine strips gives a delicious sour bite to the shrimp scampi. Saffron rice, sauteed spinach leaves, fresh broccoli, sauteed peeled cherry tomatoes, or stuffed zucchini would go very well with this dish.*

¾ cup fish stock (page 9)

¼ cup creme fraiche (page 49)

10 tablespoons butter
⅓ pound sorrel
24 large fresh shrimp, peeled and deveined, tail ends left
    on
Salt
Freshly ground white pepper
1 garlic clove, minced
¼ cup dry white wine
4 egg yolks
¼ cup heavy cream
1 tablespoon fine-chopped parsley

Remove center veins and stems from sorrel; rinse with cold water. Cut into fine julienne strips.

In two tablespoons of the butter saute sorrel over low heat for four to five minutes. Set aside to cool.

Season shrimp with salt and pepper; then saute lightly with the garlic in a large skillet in the remaining butter for eight to ten minutes. Remove from skillet and keep warm.

Add fish stock and wine to skillet and, boiling over high heat, reduce by one-third. Lower heat, add creme fraiche, and simmer for two to three minutes.

Lightly beat egg yolks with heavy whipping cream. At lowest heat, drizzle in egg mixture, whisking constantly until sauce is thickened. Do not let sauce boil. Add sorrel and salt and pepper to taste.

Place six shrimp on each serving plate and spoon sauce over them. Sprinkle with parsley.

*Suggested Wines*
   Callaway Chenin Blanc
   Grand Cru Chenin Blanc


## SCAMPI PERI-PERI
# Hot Spiced Shrimp
*Serves 4*

*I discovered the marvelous spice peri-peri when I was a chef in South Africa, and as far as I know I am the only person using it professionally in the United States today, because I had to have fifty pounds of it flown in specially for me! A hot, reddish powder, it bites the tongue and then disappears suddenly without burning—a wonderful sensation. If, like me, you tried it once and can't live without it, I will consider selling you a little of my own private store. Serve this dish with risotto or rice, as well as stuffed eggplant or sauteed zucchini with tomatoes, onions, and garlic.*

   ½ cup fish stock (page 9)

   24 large shrimp, peeled and deveined, tail end left on
   Salt
   Freshly ground white pepper
   Peri-peri powder
   10 tablespoons butter
   2 garlic cloves, minced
   1 shallot, fine-chopped

Juice from ½ lemon
1 tablespoon chopped parsley

Season shrimp with salt and pepper, and lightly with peri-peri powder.

Saute shrimp in large skillet in seven tablespoons of the butter and garlic for eight to ten minutes. Remove from skillet and keep warm. Add shallots and saute for three to four minutes; do not brown. Add ¼ teaspoon peri-peri powder, lemon juice, and fish stock and boil over high heat for three to four minutes. Lower heat and whisk in remaining butter, stirring constantly.

Place six shrimp on each serving plate. Mix chopped parsley into sauce and spoon over shrimp. Serve immediately.

*Suggested Wines*

Stony Hill White Riesling
San Martin Fume Blanc

## Saumon farci en Croute, Sauce de homard
## Stuffed Salmon in a Crust with Lobster Sauce
*Serves 4*

*We fill fresh baby salmon with shrimp, mushrooms, and leeks; bake it in a pastry crust; and serve it with a lobster cream sauce. Trim the puff pastry into the shape of a fish for a decorative extra touch, and serve with parsleyed boiled potatoes and a spinach or broccoli timbale.*

Puff pastry dough (page 195, double recipe)
1 to 1½ cups lobster sauce (page 46)

6-7 ounces diced (peeled and deveined) shrimp

Salt

Freshly ground white pepper

¼ carrot

½ leek, white part only

¼ stalk celery

4 mushrooms

4 tablespoons butter

4 10-ounce fresh baby salmon; cleaned and deboned, head removed

3 egg yolks

¼ cup milk

12 medium shrimp, peeled, deveined, and tail left on

*To prepare stuffed fish*

Season the diced shrimp with salt and pepper. Wash and fine dice all the vegetables; then gently saute with the shrimp in two tablespoons of the butter for four to five minutes. Do not brown. Set aside to cool.

Open salmon and lay, butterfly-style, on a cutting board, skin side down. Season with salt and pepper. Divide vegetable and shrimp mixture among the 4 salmon; placing it on one side of each fish. Fold the other side over the stuffing.

Roll puff pastry until you can cut it into four (6½ × 9 inch) rectangles. Place a stuffed salmon lengthwise on one side of each piece. Beat egg yolks with milk; brush the edges of the pastry dough with this egg wash. Fold the other side of the dough over and press to seal it around the fish.

Leaving about ¼ inch around the salmon, cut the dough into the shape of a fish, including a head and tail. Save the excess dough. Refrigerate pastry-wrapped fish for about 15 minutes, or until firm.

Remove from refrigerator and place on oiled baking sheet. Roll out the pastry scraps and cut out pieces to represent fins, eyes, and gill openings. Brush edges of these pieces with egg wash and attach them to the fish. Using a spoon, press half-circles into the pastry to represent scales. Brush the pastry with egg wash so it will brown nicely. Bake in a preheated 350-375°F oven for 15 to 20 minutes.

*To prepare sauce and serve*

While fish is baking, warm lobster sauce. Season medium shrimp with salt and pepper, and saute in the remaining butter over medium heat for four to five minutes.

Spoon sauce onto the serving plates. Lay one salmon on top and garnish with three shrimp around each fish.

*Suggested Wines*

>Grgich Hill Chardonnay
>Mirassou Chardonnay

## filet de Rouget a la maison
## Red Snapper with Mussels and Tomato Shrimp Sauce
*Serves 4*

*An outstanding dish served with poached mussels and a shrimp and tomato saffron sauce. We use the fresh Gulf snapper with its red skin, but sea bass would be an excellent substitute.*

>1 cup fish stock (page 9)
>
>16 poached mussels, out of the shell, bearded; strain and save stock (page 21)
>4 puff pastry half-moons (page 195)
>⅓ cup creme fraiche (page 49)
>
>7 tablespoons butter
>2 shallots, chopped fine
>4 7-ounce filets of fresh red snapper

Salt
Freshly ground white pepper
½ cup dry white wine
1½ teaspoons flour
Pinch of saffron
Juice from ½ lemon
2 medium tomatoes, peeled
9-10 ounces diced (peeled and deveined) shrimp
3 egg yolks
½ cup heavy cream

Melt two tablespoons of the butter in an ovenproof skillet (large enough to hold the snapper filets in one layer). Add shallots and cook over low heat for three to four minutes, but do not brown.

Lay fish on top of shallots and sprinkle with salt and freshly ground white pepper. Add white wine and fish stock and bring to a gentle boil. Remove from heat, cover with buttered wax paper, place into preheated 350°F oven, and bake for six to eight minutes. With a slotted spatula, remove snapper. Transfer to a serving dish, cover with wax paper, and keep warm.

Boiling over high heat, reduce cooking liquid by one quarter.

Mix flour well with a tablespoon softened butter. As stock boils, whisk flour and butter mixture into stock, stirring constantly. Simmer three to four minutes; then strain through a fine sieve. Add creme fraiche and saffron; mix well. Boil gently for three more minutes. Whisk in two tablespoons of the butter bit by bit. Add lemon juice, season with salt and pepper if needed, and simmer.
Place puff pastry half-moons in a 375°F oven and bake about 15 minutes until golden brown.

Remove seed from tomatoes and dice. Season diced shrimp with salt and pepper.

In two small skillets, melt the remaining butter over medium heat. Place diced tomatoes in one of the skillets. Sprinkle with salt and pepper and saute for three to four minutes, then pour into sauce. Saute diced shrimp in the other pan for approximately the same time; add to sauce. Drain all cooking fat into the simmering sauce also.

Lightly beat egg yolks with heavy cream. Add slowly to the sauce, whisking constantly, until sauce has thickened. Keep sauce warm but do not boil.

In a small pan, heat mussels in a half cup of mussel stock (saved from poaching mussels) for three to four minutes.

Placed snapper on serving plates, top each portion with four mussels and nap with several spoonfuls of sauce. Garnish each plate with a warm fleuron.

*Suggested Wines*

Chateau St. Jean Johannisberg Riesling
Kenwood Chenin Blanc

## filet de truite farci a l'abbe
## Trout Filled with Salmon Mousse

*Serves 4*

*For each person we make two filets of fresh river trout, filled with salmon mousse, poached, and served in a light, fresh dill sauce made from the poaching liquid. The mousse can be prepared several hours ahead of time. This dish is excellent with boiled new potatoes, green asparagus tips, and spinach timbales; at the Abbey we garnish it with Beluga Malosol caviar.*

1 cup fish stock (page 9)
4 fleurons (puff pastry half-moons, page 195)
⅓ cup creme fraiche (page 49)

¼ pound deboned and skinned fresh salmon
Salt to taste
Freshly ground white pepper to taste
Touch of nutmeg
Pinch of cayenne pepper
⅔ cup heavy cream
3-4 egg whites
4 trout
5 tablespoons butter
2 shallots, fine-chopped
⅓ cup dry white wine
1½ teaspoons flour
Juice from ½ lemon
2 tablespoons fine-chopped fresh dill
3 egg yolks

Good black caviar, optional

*To prepare mousse:*

Using a blender or food processor, blend salmon thoroughly with salt, pepper, nutmeg and cayenne. Turn off machine, add half of the heavy cream and the egg whites and combine with a rubber spatula. Then mix for 15 to 20 seconds at machine's highest speed, but do not overbeat. The mixture should now be very smooth. Transfer into a bowl set into a larger bowl filled with ice. Refrigerate at least one hour.

*To prepare trout*

Remove heads and tails, skin, and debone trout. Cut in half lengthwise.

Lay trout skinned side down and spread about 1/8 inch of salmon mousse over each filet. Fold one end of each filet over so that it meets the other end. Melt two tablespoons of the butter over low heat in an ovenproof skillet large enough to hold the trout filets in one layer. Add shallots and saute for three to four minutes, but do not brown. Place filets on top of shallots and sprinkle with salt and freshly ground white pepper. Add white wine and fish stock; then bring to a quick boil. Remove from heat and cover with buttered wax paper. Now, bake six to seven minutes in a preheated 350°F oven. Then, with a slotted spatula, remove trout and transfer to a serving dish. Cover with wax paper and keep warm.

*To prepare sauce and serve*

Reduce cooking liquid over high heat to ¾ of its original volume. Thoroughly blend flour with one tablespoon softened butter and whisk this mixture into the boiling liquid. Stirring constantly, simmer three to four minutes. Then strain through a fine sieve. Add creme fraiche, mix well, and let boil gently for three more minutes. Whisk in remaining butter bit by bit. Stir in lemon juice and chopped dill. Season with salt and pepper if necessary. Continue simmering on lowest heat.

Combine egg yolks and remaining heavy cream; then drizzle into the sauce, whisking constantly, until sauce has thickened. Keep warm, but do not let boil.

Lay two filets on each serving dish and spoon sauce over trout. If desired, top each filet with a small amount of caviar. Garnish each plate with a heated fleuron and serve.

*Suggested Wines*

    Callaway Sauvignon Blanc
    Parducci Sauvignon Blanc

# ſilet δe Sole δouvre Regence
# Dover Sole Regency

*Serves 4*

*This exquisite dish is garnished with poached oysters, and served at the Abbey with salmon and scallop mousselines and a mushroom cap that has been filled with a salpicon made from diced Maine lobster. The mixture for the mousselines can be prepared ahead of time, but the rest of the preparation involves several steps carried out in quick succession. Another way to present this dish is to set a spinach timbale into the center of the plate, arranging the fish around it and garnishing as in this recipe.*

1 quart fish stock (page 9)
Salmon mousselines (page 68)
Scallop mousselines (page 68)
⅓ cup creme fraiche (page 49)
½ cup lobster sauce (page 46)

6 tablespoons butter
2 shallots, fine-chopped
⅓ cup dry white wine
Juice from 1½ lemons
Salt
Freshly ground white pepper
4 fresh Dover sole, each cut into 4 filets

4 large mushroom caps
1 boiled Maine lobster

1½ teaspoons flour
16 fresh shelled oysters, with juice
3 egg yolks
¼ cup heavy cream
8 slices truffle, optional

### To prepare filets

In a large shallow pan, saute shallots in two tablespoons of the butter until translucent, but not browned. Then add white wine, fish stock, juice from one lemon, and salt and pepper to taste. Bring to a simmer. Place filets of sole into stock and simmer for five to seven minutes. Remove sole, cover with buttered wax paper, and keep warm.

### To prepare mousselines

Bring fish stock back to a simmer. Dip a teaspoon into the boiling stock. Using this warmed teaspoon, dip from the salmon and scallop mousseline mixtures an amount approximately the size of an unshelled walnut and gently slide into the stock. Repeat this until you have four of each mousseline. Simmer for five minutes, remove from pan with slotted spoon and place with sole filets to keep warm.

### To prepare mushrooms

Wash the mushrooms well and remove the stems. In a small skillet, saute the caps in one tablespoon of the butter. Sprinkle with salt and pepper, add lemon juice and a touch of white wine. Simmer for four to five minutes, or until done.

Slice lobster tail into eight medallions and dice the rest of the meat finely. Heat the diced meat in a small amount of the lobster sauce; then fill the mushroom caps with this mixture. Keep warm.

### To prepare sauce

Strain 1½ cups fish stock through a fine strainer and reduce by gentle boiling to one cup. Mix one tablespoon softened butter with flour and stir into stock. Bring to a slow boil, stirring constantly. Gently boil for three to four minutes, still stirring. Add creme fraiche, salt and pepper to taste, and simmer for three more minutes. Drop remaining butter bit by bit into sauce, always stirring. Strain sauce; then bring back to simmer.

Meanwhile, stiffen oysters in own juice, adding a touch of fish stock by bringing to a quick simmer for 10 seconds. Heat lobster medallions also in a little fish stock.

Mix egg yolks with whipping cream; then drizzle into your sauce, stirring constantly. Bring back to a slow simmer, but do not boil.

*To serve*

Arrange four filets of sole on each serving dish. Top each with an oyster and place one of each mousseline on the plate. Also on each plate, set a filled mushroom cap and place two lobster medallions in the center of the plate. Nap each mousseline with a spoonful of heated lobster sauce, and spoon the other sauce over the sole and lobster medallions. If desired, top each mousseline with a slice of truffle. Serve immediately.

*Suggested Wines*

> Napa Wine Cellars Johannisberg Riesling
> Chalone Vineyard Chenin Blanc

tRuITE au BlEu
# Live Trout Cooked Blue
*Serves 4*

*The beautiful sky-blue color of this dish is the result of the natural coating on the skin of the live fish, killed only seconds before it is lowered into the boiling liquid. I serve it with melted butter or a horseradish cream sauce, and accompany it with fresh boiled potatoes.*

½ cup heavy cream
Grated fresh or prepared horseradish
Salt
Lemon juice
Sugar

1 stalk celery
1 onion, peeled
1 carrot
1 bunch parsley, washed
20-25 black peppercorns
4 cups vinegar

4 live trout

*To prepare sauce*

Whip cream until soft peaks form; fold in horseradish to taste. Season with salt, lemon juice, and a touch of sugar. Chill until ready to use.

*To prepare poaching liquid*

Chop cleaned vegetables into large pieces. In a large pot, bring a gallon of salted water to a boil. Add vegetables, parsley, peppercorns, and vinegar. Reduce heat and simmer for 20 minutes. Strain the liquid into a fish-poacher or high-sided, long, oval pan; discard vegetables.

*To prepare trout and serve*

Approximately 15 minutes before serving, take trout out of water and place on a cutting board sprinkled with water. Using a wooden spoon, kill each trout with a blow to the head. Slit the fish, starting near the tail and cutting to just underneath the head. Gut and wash the trout thoroughly, being careful not to remove the skin. Sprinkle trout with a little vinegar.

For a more attractive presentation, you may bend the trout so the head meets the tail. Using a large needle, insert string through the head and tail and tie together.

Bring liquid in fish poacher to a boil. Slide trout into liquid. Reduce heat and simmer gently for eight to ten minutes. After a minute of simmering, the trout will begin to turn a light sky blue due to the interaction of the coating of their skin with the vinegar.

Remove string (if used) and place trout on serving plates. Serve with horseradish sauce on the side.

*Suggested Wines*

> Spring Mountain Chardonnay
> Beringer Chardonnay

## Brochette δe Coquille St. Jacques aux Cepes
# Scallop Brochette in a Crepe with Mushrooms
*Serves 4*

*This is a special-occasion dish that will require some advance planning—but the result is worth it, a delectable crepe filled with marinated scallops and cepes mushrooms, garnished with medallions of lobster tail, and topped with a lobster cream sauce. The cepes can be bought dried, and then soaked in cold water for an hour before using.*

*To prepare scallops*

8 bamboo skewers, 6 inches long
40-48 fresh bay scallops (about 1 pound)
1 cup olive oil
Thyme, 1 sprig fresh leaves or ¼ teaspoon dried
Bay leaves, 3 fresh or 2 dried
2 cloves garlic, minced

Place five or six scallops on each bamboo skewer and marinate in the olive oil, thyme, bay leaves, and garlic for four hours.

*To prepare lobster*

1 celery stalk
1 carrot
1 onion, peeled
Salt
2 teaspoons crushed black pepper
2 live lobsters, 1½ pounds each

Wash celery and carrot; chop these and the onion into large pieces. Add to a gallon of salted water in a large (lobster) pot with the crushed pepper. Bring to a boil and boil for 10 to 15 minutes. Plunk in live lobsters, bring to boil again, and simmer on lowest heat for 12 to 15 minutes. Remove lobsters and allow to cool. Discard broth.

Once cool, remove the meat from the lobsters. First, pull off the claws and then, tear the lobsters in half where the tail and body meet. Pull off the tail and turn tail soft side up. Trim away shell on both sides with a knife or scissors so that the meat can be removed. Slice each tail into eight "medallions," remove veins, and set aside. Crack the claws and the arms with a lobster or nut cracker. Pull out the meat and save for another dish, such as a luncheon salad. Reserve the lobster legs for a garnish.

*To serve*

   1 cup lobster cream sauce (page 46)
   8 crepes (pages 196–97)

   1 shallot, chopped fine
   ¾ cup fine-chopped cepes (or regular) mushrooms
   3 tablespoons butter
   Salt
   Freshly ground white pepper
   1 teaspoon fine-chopped fresh chives
   Parmesan cheese, grated
   2 tablespoons fine-chopped parsley
   Lobster legs (crawlers)
   Watercress
   8 lemon wedges

Saute shallots and mushrooms briefly in one tablespoon of the butter. Sprinkle with salt, pepper, and chives, mix well, and cook gently for two or three more minutes. Keep warm.

Bring lobster cream sauce to a boil and keep hot.

Remove scallop brochette from marinade. Drain all excess oil and season with salt and pepper. Saute in remaining butter over high heat in a large skillet for two or three minutes on each side, until done, but not overcooked.

Place one skewer of scallops on each crepe; then remove the skewer. Top with a spoonful of mushrooms, roll together, and place two crepes on each individual serving dish. Set two lobster medallions on each crepe. Cover crepe and lobster with lobster cream sauce, sprinkle with Parmesan cheese, and heat in a 375°F oven for two or three minutes. Then glaze under a broiler until cheese is lightly browned. Sprinkle with chopped parsley and decorate with lobster legs, watercress, and lemon wedge. Serve immediately.

*Suggested Wines*

Lambret Bridge Chardonnay
Geyser Peak Chardonnay

## filet de pompano Cleopatra
## Pompano with Shrimp, Capers, and Lemon
*Serves 4*

*Fresh pompano from Florida has a firm, somewhat oily flesh with a delicate taste; in this recipe one might substitute sole, snapper, or almost any other good fish. We serve it with fresh boiled potatoes, Brussels sprouts, or creamed yellow squash.*

4 7-ounce fresh pompano filets
Salt
Freshly ground white pepper
Worcestershire sauce
Flour
7 tablespoons butter
½ pound diced, (peeled and deveined) shrimp
2 tablespoons capers
1 lemon, cut into membrane-free segments and diced
1 tablespoon chopped fresh parsley
2 tablespoons dry white wine
Squeeze of lemon juice

Sprinkle both sides of pompano with salt, pepper, and a touch of worcestershire sauce. Flour very lightly, shaking off any excess.

Heat 5 tablespoons of the butter in large skillet until foaming. Saute filets for six to eight minutes on each side. Remove fish from skillet and keep warm.

Drain the cooking fat and heat the remaining butter in the same skillet until lightly browned. Add shrimp, seasoned with salt and pepper, and saute for three to four minutes. Add capers and diced lemon segments and briefly saute. Add chopped parsley, white wine, and squeeze of lemon juice.

Place fish on four serving dishes and spoon pan juices over fish.

*Suggested Wines*

Trefethen Vineyards Chardonnay
Rutherford Hill Chardonnay

## homard a la newbourg
## Lobster Newburg
*Serves 2*

*This classic dish is always popular at the Abbey. Serve it with saffron rice accompanied by fresh asparagus or sauteed champignon mushrooms.*

½ cup fish stock (page 9)

1 stalk celery
1 carrot
1 medium onion, peeled
1 leek, white part only
Salt
18-20 crushed peppercorns
2 lemons, cut in half
1 tablespoon pickling spice
2 Maine lobsters, 1¾ to 2 pounds each
1 tablespoon butter
1 tablespoon olive oil
2 tablespoons cognac
¼ cup Madeira wine
Freshly ground white pepper
Cayenne pepper
½ cup heavy cream
3 egg yolks

Wash vegetables (except onions) and chop into large pieces. Place in a pot (large enough for lobsters) with peppercorns, lemons, pickling spice, and a half gallon of salted water. Boil for 15 minutes. Add lobsters to boiling stock; bring to a boil again. Turn off heat and let sit for about eight minutes. Remove lobsters and discard stock.

Remove meat from lobster claws and tail and slice one-half inch thick.

Heat butter and oil in a large shallow pan. Saute lobster meat lightly, but do not brown. Pour cognac over lobster meat and flame. Then add Madeira wine and, boiling gently, reduce to one-third the volume. Add fish stock, a dash of salt and pepper, and a touch of cayenne pepper. Bring to a gentle boil; then simmer for five minutes.

Lightly beat cream with egg yolks and pour over lobster. On lowest heat, warm mixture slowly, stirring constantly, until sauce thickens. Do not boil. Correct seasonings if needed and serve.

*Suggested Wines*

　　Chateau St. Jean Chardonnay
　　Sebastiani Chardonnay

# fowl and Game Birds

FRESH, YOUNG, TENDER BIRD is the first require-
ment of a fine poultry or game bird dish. When I buy for
the Abbey, I am always alert to offers of fresh pheasant,
pigeons, or other game birds that are usually only
available frozen; and the home chef can watch for local specialties
as well, when they are in season. When you obtain fresh game
birds, though, be especially careful not to destroy their protective
layer of fat just under the skin by washing it off. Not only does the
fat provide the only natural basting liquid for the bird, but it also
protects against the bacteria that can cause game birds to spoil
quite easily. Simply pat the bird dry with paper towels after you
have extracted the innards, and take care that it is well refrigerated
both before and after the feast.

Game birds lend themselves most easily to the elaborate
presentations that delight the eye. One of my favorite recipes in this
chapter is for the quail "a la Vigneronne." The tiny birds nest in a
bed of sauerkraut flavored with champagne and fresh pineapple,
all within a rectangular enclosure of puff pastry shell; and peeled,

sauteed grapes, like little eggs, add the final imaginative garnish. Another versatile recipe'is the poached stuffed breast of chicken, which provides endless possibilities for variation depending on what is in season or in your larder.

## Oie Rotie a la Suedoise
## Swedish Roast Goose
*Serves 8 to 10*

*This luscious roast goose is garnished with sauteed grapes and served with a stuffed apple and cooked red cabbage. The sauce is clear and thin, flavored with the bones and drippings as well as rosemary and thyme. Do not thicken it with flour; a touch of arrowroot or cornstarch will give it a nice shine as well as slightly thickening it. I like to accompany roast goose with Salade Capri and parsleyed boiled potatoes; the salad and the stuffed apple can be prepared ahead, and the red cabbage marinated hours before you will need it.*

8-10 stuffed apples (page 164)
Salade Capri (page 164—double all amounts)
Red cabbage (page 172)
1 cup brown stock (page 4) or beef stock (page 5)

1 goose, 10-12 pounds
1 stalk celery
1 carrot
1 onion, peeled
1 leek, white part only
Salt
Freshly ground white pepper
Rosemary, 2 sprigs fresh leaves or ½ teaspoon dried
⅓ cup dry white wine
1 sprig fresh  thyme or ¼ teaspoon dried
Bay leaves, 3 fresh or 2 dried
1 tablespoon cornstarch or arrowroot

1 pound seedless grapes, peeled
1½ teaspoons sugar
1 tablespoon butter

Wash vegetables (except onion) and chop into large pieces.

Remove neck and innards from goose. Set aside liver for another dish. Place neck and remaining innards in a roasting pan with the vegetables. Do not wash goose, but dry thoroughly with paper towel. Sprinkle salt, pepper, and half of the rosemary inside goose. Rub salt and pepper thoroughly into the skin of the goose.

Set goose into pan with vegetables. Add two to three cups of water and roast goose, basting frequently, at 350°F for 2½ to 3 hours. Remove goose from pan and keep warm.

Add brown (or beef) stock and wine to roasting pan with vegetables. Add remaining rosemary, and the thyme and bay leaves; simmer for 10 to 15 minutes. Season with salt and pepper. Skim grease from pan juices. Mix cornstarch with a little cold water and stir it into simmering sauce to thicken. Strain through a fine sieve.

Sprinkle peeled grapes with sugar and saute in butter for two to three minutes.

Separate breast and legs from goose. Debone legs and slice leg meat. Lay slices on individual serving plates. Slice breast one quarter inch thick; layer on top of the leg slices. Ladle sauce over meat. Arrange six to eight sauteed grapes on top of each serving. Garnish each plate with a braised apple. Serve with Salade Capri, red cabbage, and boiled potatoes.

*Suggested Wines*

Spring Mountain Cabernet Sauvignon
San Martin Cabernet Sauvignon

# fAISAn ROTI SOUVAROff
## Roast Pheasant in Madeira Sauce
*Serves 4*

*This is one of the traditional French game bird dishes, and a favorite at the Abbey. It is served with Madeira sauce and garnished with a pate made of goose liver and truffles, although you can substitute button mushrooms for the truffles. You will need one to four deep covered casseroles to hold the four pheasants.*

> 1 cup demi-glace (page 6)
> 2 pounds puff pastry dough (page 195)
>
> 4 pheasants, 1-1¼ pounds each
> Salt
> Freshly ground white pepper
> 4 slices fatback (pork fat), 1/8 inch thick and 4 × 5 inches
> 8 tablespoons butter
> 1-2 shallots, chopped fine
> ⅓ cup Madeira wine
> 8 pieces goose liver
> 1 fine-chopped truffle, optional
> 4 ounces diced pate de fois gras
> 2 eggs
> ¼ cup light cream

Remove innards from pheasant and discard. Do not wash pheasant, but dry with paper towels. Season with salt and pepper. Tuck wings under each pheasant. Lay one piece of fatback over each pheasant and secure with string.

Heat six tablespoons of the butter in a large ovenproof skillet or roasting pan. Place pheasants into skillet on one side (not top or bottom). Brown by turning frequently from one side to the other. Place into preheated 350°F oven and roast for approximately 20 minutes, basting occasionally. Pheasant will be slightly undercooked. Remove from pan and keep warm.

Drain half of the butter from pan and return to stove top. Add shallots and saute slowly for three to four minutes. Deglaze with Madeira wine. Add demi-glace and let simmer.

Untie pheasants, discard fat and string, and debone. Using a meat cleaver or heavy French knife, cut bones into approximately one-inch pieces and add them to the sauce. Continue to simmer for 10 to 15 minutes.

Clean goose liver and season with salt and pepper. Heat one tablespoon of the butter in a skillet and saute goose liver for three to four minutes. Remove liver and keep warm with pheasant.

Strain sauce through a fine sieve. Whisk in remaining butter bit by bit.

Place each pheasant into a deep individual casserole or place all four in one large casserole. Top each pheasant with chopped truffles, diced pate de fois gras, and two pieces goose liver. Pour equal amounts of sauce into each casserole. Cover and seal the edge of each casserole with a ring of puff pastry dough. Mix eggs with cream and brush puff pastry with this egg wash. Bake at 350°F for 10 to 15 minutes. To serve, break crust(s) gently and serve some with the meat.

*Suggested Wines*

Stag's Leap Wine Cellars Cabernet Sauvignon
Parducci Cabernet Sauvignon

Cailles Roties a la Vigneronne
# Roast Quail with Grapes and Champagne Kraut
*Serves 4*

*Within a rectangular puff pastry shell, three tiny quail nest in a bed of champagne pineapple sauerkraut, with sauteed grapes as a garnish. This is an enchanting dish both to the eye and to the palate.*

> 1 cup demi-glace (page 6)
> 1 recipe champagne kraut with pineapple (page 174)
> Puff pastry dough (page 195, double recipe)
>
> 12 quail, each 4 to 4½ ounces
> Salt
> Freshly ground white pepper
> 12 slices fatback, each 1/8 inch thick and 3 × 2½ inches
> 10 tablespoons butter
> ½ cup dry white wine
> 1 pound seedless white grapes, peeled
> 1 tablespoon sugar

## To prepare pastry shells

Divide puff pastry into four equal pieces. Roll each into a rectangle measuring five inches by seven inches. Trim a one-inch strip from all four sides; lay these on top of the remaining rectangle to form four walls, trimming any extending pieces. You do not need to press or pinch the dough; it will fuse together in the oven. Bake at 350°F for 30 minutes, or until golden brown.

## To prepare quail and serve

Do not wash the quail, but remove innards and dry birds with paper towels. Season with salt and pepper. Lay one slice of fatback atop each bird and secure with string.

Heat three tablespoons of the butter in a large ovenproof skillet or roasting pan. When butter is foaming, place quail into pan and brown on all sides, turning every three to four minutes. Then, bake in a preheated 350°F oven for 15 to 20 minutes, basting frequently. Remove from pan; untie and discard fatback. Set quail aside and keep warm.

Deglaze the pan with white wine. Add demi-glace and simmer for five to eight minutes. Strain and keep warm.

Heat champagne kraut with pineapple. Warm pastry shells in a slow oven.

Saute grapes in remaining butter for three to four minutes; sprinkle with sugar.

Place a pastry shell on each plate and fill with kraut. Set three quail into each shell on top of the kraut. Nap each quail with a tablespoon or two of the sauce; top with sauteed grapes. Serve immediately.

*Suggested Wines*

> Mondavi Cabernet Sauvignon
> Rutherford Hill Chardonnay

## Canarò Roti au Poivre Vert
# Roast Duckling with Green Peppercorns
*Serves 4*

*The briny green peppercorns from Madagascar give a mild but distinctly hot taste to this roast duckling dish. Allow time to debone the cooked duck before you make the sauce. Snow peas, sauteed green beans, and broccoli polonaise go very well with this dish.*

> ½ cup demi-glace (page 6)

2 4- to 4½-pound ducklings
½ cup dry red wine
2 tablespoons green peppercorns in brine (not in vinegar)

Prepare and roast ducks as for roast duck with fresh fruit (page 130), except do not use orange quarters. Remove ducks from pan and rest for five to ten minutes; then untie. Remove breast and legs from ducks; debone completely. Save bones for sauce and keep meat warm.

*To prepare sauce*

Skim all fat from roasting pan and discard. Retain vegetables and duck juices. Deglaze pan with red wine and bring to a boil. Add bones and boil for several minutes; then add demi-glace and a tablespoon of green peppercorns. Simmer for 10 to 15 minutes; then strain through a fine sieve. Add remaining peppercorns and keep hot.

Slice leg meat ¼ inch thick and arrange on individual serving plates. Slice each breast diagonally lengthwise, also ¼ inch thick, and layer them on top of the leg meat. Spoon hot sauce over all and serve.

*Suggested Wines*

Kenwood "Jack London" Cabernet Sauvignon
Firestone Cabernet Sauvignon

## Canard Roti aux Fruits d'Or
# Roast Duckling with Fresh Fruit
*Serves 4*

*A classic bigarade sauce accompanies this roast duck, as well as poached fresh peach halves, fresh orange sections, and peeled, sliced kiwi fruit. The sauce is prepared at the last minute, after deboning the cooked duck.*

> 2½ cups bigarade sauce (page 38), made with bones from this roast duck
>
> 2 4- to 4½-pound ducklings
> Salt
> Freshly ground black pepper
> 1 stalk celery
> 1 carrot
> 2 onions, peeled
> 2 unpeeled oranges
> 12 orange segments
> 4 peach halves
> Lemon juice
> 12 slices kiwi

Remove any extra fat underneath the skin and the neck of the duck. Set the innards aside and wash duck inside and out; dry with paper towels. Cut away neck skin. Season inside and out with salt and pepper.

Tie the duck with butcher's string: Starting at the duck's ankle, twist the string around one foot, then the other, and then around both. Pass string between ankles and wrap it around the duck lengthwise three times; then wrap it three times around the width of the duck and tie securely. The duck will now look like a wrapped package!

Chop celery, carrot, and onions into large pieces. Quarter the unpeeled oranges.

Spread vegetables, orange quarters, and innards over the bottom of a roasting pan. Add three cups of water. Place a wire rack on top of vegetables and set the trussed ducks on top. Roast in a preheated 375-400°F oven until done and skin is crisp, about 1¼ to 1½ hours. While roasting, turn duck two or three times. Leave duck breast-side up for the last 30 minutes of roasting.

While roasting, poach peeled peach halves in sugared water for two to three minutes. Drain and sprinkle with lemon juice. Remove all membranes from orange segments. Keep orange and kiwi cold; saute peach halves briefly in butter just before serving.

Remove ducks from pan and rest for five to ten minutes. Untie and separate breasts and legs. Carefully remove bones for sauce and chop into two-inch pieces with a meat cleaver or heavy French knife. Put meat aside and keep warm.

Strain the drippings and juices from the pan into a bowl. Skim off the grease and discard. Save juices for sauce.

Prepare bigarade sauce (page 38), using the bones from this duck.

Arrange portions of duckling (one leg and one breast per person) on individual serving plates and decorate with orange segments, kiwi, and sauteed peach halves. Spoon on sauce and serve immediately.

*Suggested Wines*

>Clos du Bois Cabernet Sauvignon
>Beringer Cabernet Sauvignon

## Supreme de Volaille au Poireau et Cressonette
## Breast of Chicken with Leek and Watercress

*Serves 4*

*The boneless breast of chicken is filled with fine vegetables, poached, and covered with a sauce made with leeks and watercress. Leave the wingbone to the first joint attached, both for decorative reasons and to hold it together as it is filled. We serve two breasts for each person, accompanied by rice and a spinach timbale. The vegetable filling can be prepared ahead to save time.*

1 quart chicken stock (page 8)
⅓ cup creme fraiche (page 49)

*To prepare stuffing*

¼ carrot
1 onion
½ stalk celery
½ leek, white part only
4-5 mushrooms
½ bunch watercress leaves
2 tablespoons butter

Wash the carrot, celery, leek, mushrooms, and watercress; chop these and the onion fine. Saute carrot, onion, and celery in the butter over medium heat for three to four minutes; do not brown. Add leek, mushrooms, and watercress and a touch of water. Cook gently for four to five minutes more. Set aside to cool.

*To prepare chicken breasts*

4 8-ounce boneless chicken breasts, with wingbone to first joint attached
Salt
Freshly ground white pepper

Lightly pound breasts with a mallet until thin. Lay flattened breasts on a flat surface, inside of breast up, and season with salt and pepper. Divide vegetable stuffing, placing it down the center of each breast. Roll breast lengthwise and tie securely with string so that stuffing cannot fall out. Tying this rolled breast as though it were a package works well, crossing the lengthwise and crosswise string at one-inch intervals.

Bring chicken stock to a boil, add stuffed breast, and simmer for 12 to 15 minutes. Remove breasts, untie, and keep warm. Save stock.

*To prepare sauce and serve*

> 4 tablespoons butter
> 1 shallot, chopped fine
> ⅓ cup fine-chopped leek, white part only
> ⅓ cup fine-chopped watercress leaves
> 1½ teaspoons flour
> ¼ cup dry white wine
> ¾ chicken stock, saved above
> Salt
> Freshly ground white pepper
> 3 egg yolks
> 1 tablespoon chopped fresh parsley

In a saucepan, saute shallot, leek, and watercress for two to three minutes in two tablespoons of the butter; do not brown. Sprinkle in flour and stir well. Add wine and chicken stock; simmer for five to eight minutes. Stir in creme fraiche and season with salt and pepper. Whisk in remaining butter bit by bit; simmer for two to three minutes more.

Lightly beat egg yolks in a small bowl. Slowly whisk in several spoonfuls of the hot sauce; drizzle this warmed egg yolk mixture back into the sauce, stirring constantly. Let simmer gently for two minutes, still stirring.

Lay stuffed chicken breasts on individual serving plates. Spoon sauce over the meat, sprinkle with parsley, and serve immediately.

*Suggested Wines*

> Mondavi Chenin Blanc
> Dry Creek Chenin Blanc

## Supreme de Volaille au Porto
## Breast of Chicken in Port Wine

*Serves 4*

*Sauteed boneless breast of chicken is braised in a port wine cream sauce, and served with sliced sauteed apples and toasted almonds, rice and vegetables. For decoration, leave the wingbone to the first joint attached.*

½ cup demi-glace (page 6)
⅓ cup creme fraiche (page 49)

4 7- to 8-ounce skinned boneless chicken breasts, with
    wingbone to first joint attached
Salt
Freshly ground white pepper
Flour
8 tablespoons butter
2 shallots, chopped fine
½ cup port wine
2-3 bay leaves
½ tablespoon green peppercorns, in brine
20 skinless apple slices, about ½ inch thick
2 tablespoons sliced almonds, lightly browned

Clean wingbone of all fat and skin. Lightly flatten chicken breasts with a mallet; season with salt and pepper and flour lightly. Shake off any excess flour.

In a large skillet, brown chicken breasts on both sides in half of the butter. Add shallots and saute for two to three minutes. Add port wine, demi-glace, bay leaves, and peppercorns. Cover and cook slowly for about 10 minutes. Remove chicken and keep warm. Strain sauce through a fine sieve, add creme fraiche and return to heat to simmer.

In another skillet, saute apple slices in two tablespoons of the butter for three to five minutes or until soft.

Now whisk in remaining butter bit by bit. Season sauce with salt and freshly ground pepper. Place chicken breasts on serving dishes, spoon with sauce, and sprinkle hot almond slices on top. Decorate with five apple slices around each breast and serve immediately.

*Suggested Wines*

Mondavi Gamay Rose
Sebastiani (Eye of the Swan) Pinot Blanc

# meat and Game

OR THE GOURMET who wishes to cook meat at home, a good relationship with an excellent butcher is an essential element of success. The commercial butcher in most cases is simply not accustomed to cutting meat after the fashion of a restaurant kitchen, and you will have to make special requests for your tenderloins of veal and pork, your boned and trimmed lamb rib chops, your medallions, tournedos, and noisettes. Persevere; for the difference between a properly trimmed cut and a supermarket steak can be the difference between the sublime and the absurd.

At the same time, I believe that the less commonly prepared meats—which are usually less expensive as well—such as organ meats, sweetbreads, shoulder, and the like, can be as delicate and sumptuous as the most expensive tenderloin. Those who turn up their noses at such simple fare, whether in a restaurant or at home, are missing the opportunity to sample some of the world's classic dishes.

Game meats, too, provide an elegant basis for gourmet meals; and the home chef will often have the opportunity to obtain them fresh during the season from a friend who is a hunter. Remember that game meats are always improved with the addition of juniper berries to the recipe; their wild, piquant flavor is just the right complement to the strong game taste.

## Filet de Boeuf Flambe a la Russe
## Filet of Beef Flamed with Vodka
*Serves 4*

*The Indonesian spice* Sambal Oelec *gives this dish a wonderful hot taste that does not burn the tongue, and the Russian vodka with which it is flamed adds a special flair. If beef tenderloin is unavailable, any tender cut of steak suitable for sauteing will make a fine substitute. Serve with fresh vegetables, Duchesse potatoes, or buttered homemade noodles; but stay away from creamed vegetables because the sauce is already very creamy.*

½ cup demi-glace (page 6)
¼ cup creme fraiche (page 49)

4 tenderloin steaks, about 8 ounces each
Salt
Freshly ground white pepper
5 tablespoons butter
2 tablespoons vodka (100 proof)
1 medium onion, peeled and chopped fine
½ cup thin-sliced mushrooms
1 clove garlic, minced
¼ cup julienne of cornichons (or pickles)
1 tablespoon prepared brown, seedless mustard
Pinch of Sambal Oelek

Butterfly steaks by slicing almost all the way through lengthwise and spreading the two pieces apart. Flatten slightly with a mallet and season on both sides with salt and pepper. Heat three tablespoons of the butter in a large skillet over high heat. When butter is foaming, saute steaks for three to four minutes on each side (for medium rare). Pour vodka over steaks and flame either by tilting the skillet over your gas burner to catch the flame into the pan or by simply lighting a match and holding it over the pan. Remove skillet from heat, place steaks on platter, and keep warm.

Add the remaining butter to the skillet, return to medium heat, add onions, and saute until translucent, about three minutes. Then add mushrooms and garlic and saute for three more minutes, stirring frequently. Stir in cornichons, mustard, Sambal Oelek, and demi-glace; bring to a boil, then simmer for three to four minutes. Add salt and pepper to taste, mix in creme fraiche, and keep hot.

Place steaks on individual serving plates, pour any accumulated juices into the sauce, spoon sauce over steaks, and serve.

*Suggested Wines*

Beaulieu Vineyard "Caneros Creek" Pinot Noir
Louis Martini Pinot Noir

# filet δε Boeuf Roti fRascati
## Roast Tenderloin of Beef with Truffles and Pate

*Serves 4 to 6*

*This whole roasted tenderloin is topped with sauce and served with the classic "Frascati" accompaniments of truffles, mushrooms, and pate de foie gras. We serve fresh green asparagus and stuffed artichoke bottoms on the side. Note that you will need a special needle to lard the tenderloin and give it additional flavor; look for this in a gourmet specialty store.*

¾ cup demi-glace (page 6)
6 large stuffed mushroom caps (page 177)

1 whole tenderloin of beef, trimmed
¾ pound fresh pork fat for larding the filet
Salt
Freshly ground black pepper
7 tablespoons butter
2 shallots, chopped fine
1 clove garlic, minced
⅓ cup dry red wine
2 fresh (or canned) truffles, chopped fine

6 slices pate de foie gras
18 small round canapes; 6 decorated with smoked salmon, 6 with caviar, and 6 with lobster medallions

Slice off head and tail ends of the tenderloin and save for another dish. Cut lard into narrow strips about two inches long.

Using a larding needle and beginning at the front of the loin and working toward the tail end, stitch strips of lard into the meat by inserting the needle and bringing it out again about ½-inch from the point of entry. Hold onto the fat when you remove the needle so that the fat strips remain in the filet. When finished, you should have at least three rows running from front to tail across the width of the tenderloin. Season the larded tenderloin with salt and pepper.

In an ovenproof skillet large enough to hold the tenderloin, melt four tablespoons of the butter over high heat. When butter is foaming, add tenderloin and sear on all sides. Then transfer skillet with meat into a preheated 400°F oven and cook for about 15 minutes, turning frequently. (Cooking time depends on thickness of meat and desired degree of doneness.) Remove meat to a platter and keep warm.

Drain half of the fat from the skillet; add one tablespoon fresh butter and the shallots, and saute for three to four minutes until translucent, but not browned. Then add garlic and deglaze skillet with red wine. Add demi-glace and salt and pepper to taste. Simmer for 10 minutes. Whip in remaining butter bit by bit and then add chopped truffles, small amount of the truffle juice (if using canned truffles), and any accumulated juice from the tenderloin.

Carve three slices of meat for each serving and place in layers on each plate. Spoon sauce over meat and arrange strips of pate de fois gras on top of that. Lay one stuffed mushroom cap beside the meat on each plate. Decorate edge of each plate with three assorted canapes. Serve immediately.

*Suggested Wines*

Chateau Montelena Cabernet Sauvignon
Inglenook Cabernet Sauvignon

## ENTRECOTE AU POIVRE VERT
# Strip Loin Steak with Mustard and Green Peppercorn Sauce

*Serves 8*

*I use green peppercorns preserved in brine in the mustard cream sauce that accompanies this dish, which can be made with any tender cut of steak.*

¾ cup demi-glace (page 6)
2-3 tablespoons creme fraiche (page 49)

8 well-trimmed strip loin steaks, 10 to 12 ounces each
Salt
Freshly ground black pepper
5 tablespoons green peppercorns, in brine
⅓ cup prepared brown, seedless mustard
7 tablespoons butter
4 tablespoons olive oil
2-3 shallots, chopped fine
⅓ cup dry white wine
⅓ cup heavy cream
2 cloves garlic, minced
2 tablespoons fine-chopped parsley

Season the steaks with salt and pepper. Using your fingers, press half of the peppercorns into the meat; then spread both sides of the steaks very thinly with half of the mustard.

Heat two tablespoons of the butter and two tablespoons of the olive oil in each of two large skillets. When hot, sear steaks for two minutes on each side. Lower heat and cook for a total of seven to ten minutes for medium rare, actual cooking time depending on the thickness of the steaks. Remove from the skillet and keep warm on a plate.

Drain the fat from one pan; then deglaze with the white wine and save. Into the other skillet, add chopped shallots and saute until translucent, but not browned. Add the remaining mustard and peppercorns, stir well, then add whipping cream. Pour the wine from the deglazed pan into the cream, add garlic, and simmer for three minutes. Then add demi-glace, stir well, and simmer five more minutes. Season with salt and pepper. Beat in remaining butter bit by bit. Add creme fraiche and stir well. Add any juices accumulated from the steaks and mix in the chopped parsley.

Place steaks on individual serving dishes. Bring sauce to a quick boil, then spoon over steaks.

*Suggested Wines*

> Clos du Val Cabernet Sauvignon
> Beaulieu Vineyard Cabernet Sauvignon

## Boeuf Emince Nicoise
## Tenderloin Strips in Tomatoes and Garlic
*Serves 6 to 8*

*A simple, easily prepared dish that I discovered while improvising a Sunday brunch at home, this is a good use for the ends and trimmings from a tenderloin roast or other tender cut. If you have a Burgundy sauce on hand, you can use it in place of demi-glace and red wine. I serve this with homemade buttered noodles and fresh vegetables such as haricots verts wrapped in bacon, spinach timbale, or glazed baby carrots.*

1 cup demi-glace (page 6)

2½ pounds beef tenderloin, totally trimmed
Salt
Freshly ground black pepper
5 tablespoons butter

2 tablespoons olive oil
½ pound fresh mushrooms, diced
2-3 tomatoes; peeled, seeds removed, and diced
2 garlic cloves, minced
2-3 bay leaves
½ cup dry red wine
2 tablespoons fine-chopped parsley
6 tablespoons grated Parmesan cheese

Slice meat into strips, 1½ to 2 inches long and ½ to ¾ inch thick.

Season the strips with salt and pepper. Heat three tablespoons of the butter and all of the oil in a large skillet with high sides. (If you do not have a skillet large enough for all the meat to lie flat on the bottom, use either two smaller skillets or cook the meat in two steps.) When oil and butter are hot, sear the meat over high heat for about five minutes, turning frequently so that meat will brown on every surface. Turn off heat and remove meat with a slotted spoon to a bowl.

Return skillet to medium heat, add shallots, and saute until translucent. Add mushrooms and saute for three to four minutes more, stirring so that shallots and mushrooms will not stick to the pan. Add diced tomatoes, garlic, and bay leaves; season with salt and pepper. Saute for three to four minutes. Then add red wine and demi-glace and simmer 8-10 minutes more. Whip in remaining two tablespoons of butter bit by bit, simmer three more minutes, and then add parsley. Turn off heat. Add the meat to the sauce with any accumulated juices. Correct seasonings if necessary.

Spoon equal portions onto individual serving dishes, sprinkle with Parmesan cheese, and broil quickly until browned.

*Suggested Wines*

Jordan Vineyard Cabernet Sauvignon
Martin Ray "La Montana" Pinot Noir

## tournedos Quirinal
## Tournedos of Beef Tenderloin

*Serves 4*

*Two decorative little towers of elegance, based on the tournedos that have been cut from the tenderloin just at the point where it begins to narrow, but before the ends. The dish consists of layers, starting with a crouton and topping it with prosciutto, beef, sauce, a mushroom cap, and a morsel of poached bone marrow. (Your butcher can remove the marrow for you intact.) Note that the bearnaise sauce is best made just before it is needed, as it does not store well.*

¼ cup demi-glace (page 6)
½ cup bearnaise sauce (page 45)
2 tablespoons creme fraiche (page 49)

1½ to 1¾ pounds trimmed beef tenderloin
6 tablespoons butter
2 shallots, chopped fine
1 clove garlic, minced
1½ tablespoons prepared brown, seedless mustard
2½ tablespoons dry white wine
2½ tablespoons heavy cream
Juice of ½ lemon
Salt
Freshly ground white pepper

8 thin slices prosciutto ham
8 white mushroom caps, washed and stems removed
¼ pound beef marrow, diced
8 white bread rounds, each 2- to-2½ inches in diameter

Prepare bearnaise sauce as directed on page 45.

Slice the tenderloin into one-inch thick rounds; season these "tournedos" with salt and pepper. Heat two tablespoons of the butter in each of two large skillets over high heat. When butter is foaming, put four tournedos into each pan, reduce heat, and saute three to four minutes on each side (or to your liking). Remove from skillet and keep warm.

In one of the skillets, saute shallots three to four minutes, but do not brown. Mix in garlic and mustard. Add white wine, heavy cream, demi-glace, and half of the lemon juice; season with salt and pepper. Let simmer.

In the other skillet, lightly saute the prosciutto ham on both sides over low heat.

In a third skillet, melt a tablespoon of butter and saute the mushroom caps over medium heat. Sprinkle with salt and pepper, add the remaining lemon juice, and simmer for four to five minutes or until mushrooms are done. Set aside and keep warm.

Blanch marrow in boiling water for one to two minutes.

Stir the remaining butter into the mustard sauce. Add any accumulated juices from the tournedos and mix in creme fraiche.

Butter bread rounds and bake in a hot oven until browned on both sides. Place two of these croutons on each serving plate. Place a slice of prosciutto ham on top of each crouton, then lay tournedos on top of the ham. Cover one tournedo with mustard sauce and the other one with bearnaise sauce. Now set a mushroom cap on each individual tournedo and fill with the blanched marrow. Serve immediately.

*Suggested Wines*

> Heitz Cellars "Martha's Vineyard" Cabernet Sauvignon
> Clos du Bois Pinot Noir

Côte de Boeuf à la Moelle Marchand de Vin
# Rib Steak of Beef with Red Wine Sauce and Marrow

*Serves 4*

*At the Abbey we cut the meat off the bone before serving this dish, but at home you may choose to present the cut whole. Ask your butcher to cut the marrow out of the bone for you so that it will stay intact.*

½ cup demi-glace (page 6)

4 16-ounce rib steaks, including bone
Salt
Freshly ground black pepper
12 tablespoons butter
4 tablespoons olive oil
2 shallots, chopped fine
⅓ cup dry red wine
2 garlic cloves, minced
Pinch cayenne pepper
Squeeze of lemon juice
½ pound bone marrow, diced
2 tablespoons fine-chopped parsley

Trim steaks of extra fat and season with salt and pepper. Heat four tablespoons of the butter and two tablespoons of the oil in each of two large ovenproof skillets over high heat. When butter is foaming, sear the steaks on each side for two to three minutes. Place steaks (in skillets) into a preheated 400 to 425°F oven and bake, turning occasionally, for 12 to 15 minutes (for medium rare). Remove from skillets and keep warm.

Drain half of the fat from one skillet; add shallots and saute for three to four minutes. Deglaze pan with half of the wine.

Deglaze the other pan with the rest of the wine and pour this back into the pan with the shallots and simmer for three to four minutes. Add demi-glace, garlic, cayenne, and lemon juice; season with salt and pepper. Bring to a boil and simmer for eight to ten minutes.

While sauce is simmering, blanch the marrow in boiling water for one to two minutes. Whisk the remaining butter into the sauce bit by bit, then pour in any juices accumulated from the steaks. Add the blanched marrow and chopped parsley.

Remove bone from steaks and slice steaks ½-inch thick against the grain, or serve whole. Arrange individual serving plates and spoon sauce with marrow over the meat.

*Suggested Wines*

>Freemark Abbey Cabernet Sauvignon
>Sterling Cabernet Sauvignon

### Escalope de Veau Nouvelle Bertram
## Veal Cutlet Filled with Mushrooms and Herbs

*Serves 8*

*The veal cutlet should be cut from the loin, deboned, and trimmed of all fat; close to one whole side of the loin will be necessary for six people. Flattened carefully with a fine-pointed mallet, it is then filled with mushrooms and herbs, and served two to a person with a light cream sauce. I like to accompany this dish with stuffed zucchini or broccoli timbales, and homemade noodles or saffron rice.*

*To prepare stuffing and meat*

¼ cup fine-chopped scallions
2 tablespoons fine-chopped fresh sorrel
1 tablespoon fine-chopped fresh tarragon
1 onion, chopped fine
3 tablespoons butter
1 tablespoon fine-chopped parsley
1½ cup sliced mushrooms
Salt
Freshly ground white pepper
Juice from ¼ lemon
3 pounds trimmed veal loin
¼ cup flour
3 tablespoons butter

Saute scallions, sorrel, tarragon, and onion in a skillet over medium heat using one tablespoon of the butter, for two to three minutes. Then add chopped parsley and cook for one more minute. Remove from heat to cool. Melt the remaining butter in another skillet. Add mushrooms, sprinkle with salt and pepper, squeeze in lemon juice, and saute for three or four minutes. Remove from heat to cool. When both mixtures are cool, combine and drain the excess liquid.

Slice the veal loin into sixteen pieces, about three ounces each. Gently pound the veal pieces until thin; then season the flattened meat with salt and pepper. Place a spoonful of the stuffing on one side of the veal; fold the other side over to cover the stuffing. Carefully flour the stuffed veal and shake off any excess flour.

Heat three tablespoons butter in each of two large skillets. When butter is foaming, place 8 pieces of veal into each skillet and saute both sides for two to three minutes. Remove veal to a plate and keep warm. Reserve the skillets as is.

*To prepare sauce*

> 1 cup demi-glace (page 6)
> ¼ cup creme fraiche (page 49)
>
> 5 tablespoons butter
> 1-2 strips bacon, chopped fine
> 2 shallots, chopped fine
> ¾ pound fresh (or canned) chanterelle (or regular) mushrooms
> Salt
> Freshly ground white pepper
> 3 tablespoons prepared brown seedless mustard
> 2 garlic cloves, minced
> ½ cup heavy cream
> 2 tablespoons cognac
> 2 tablespoons chopped fresh parsley

Remove most of the fat from one of the skillets, add bacon, and saute for two minutes. Then add half of the shallots and saute for three to four minutes more. Add chanterelles, season with salt and pepper, mix well, and saute for five or six more minutes. Set aside.

In the other skillet, saute the remaining shallots (in the fat in which the veal was cooked) until translucent, two or three minutes. Add mustard and garlic and mix well. Add heavy cream and bring to a boil. Then, simmering four or five minutes, reduce by one third. Add demi-glace, season with salt and pepper, and simmer for several minutes. Blend in creme fraiche. As simmering continues, whip in the remaining butter bit by bit.

Arrange veal on individual serving plates, and pour any juices accumulated into the sauce. Also add cognac to the sauce, strain, then pour over chanterelles. Mix well and bring to a quick boil. Then spoon sauce over veal, sprinkle with chopped parsley, and serve immediately.

*Suggested Wines*

Gundlach-Bundschu Chardonnay
Caneros Creek Pinot Noir

## Steak δε Veau Oscar
# Veal with Crabmeat and Asparagus
*Serves 8*

*Although this is not an uncommon dish in fine restaurants, it is simple, elegant, and very popular with Abbey diners; and it can easily be prepared at home. Duchesse or Berny potatoes make a good accompaniment, as well as yellow squash souffle, peeled and sauteed cherry tomatoes, or stuffed mushroom caps.*

⅓ cup demi-glace (page 6)
½ cup bearnaise sauce (page 45)
8 pieces lightly cooked green asparagus (page 170)

6-8 tablespoons butter
8 veal loin steaks, 6 ounces each
Salt
Freshly ground white pepper

½ cup flour
8 pieces crabmeat (leg meat, about 1 ounce each, or fresh lump crabmeat)

¼ cup dry white wine
Juice from ½ lemon
2 tablespoons chopped fresh parsley

Flatten veal with a mallet to about ½ inch thick.

Heat butter in two large skillets (one should be ovenproof). Season veal with salt and pepper, then flour. Shake off any excess flour. When butter is foaming, place four veal steaks in each skillet and saute over medium to high heat for about three minutes on each side. Remove meat from skillet to a plate and keep warm.

Place the crab meat and the asparagus into one of the skillets. Warm quickly in a medium-hot oven. Deglaze the other pan with the white wine. Add demi-glace and lemon juice; bring to a boil. Pour any juice accumulated from the veal steaks into this sauce.

Spoon two tablespoons sauce on each individual serving plate and set veal steaks on top of sauce. Top each with the meat of one crab leg (or one ounce lump crabmeat) and one piece asparagus. Spoon bearnaise sauce over crabmeat, sprinkle with parsley, and serve.

*Suggested Wines:*

Chateau Chevalier Chardonnay
Callaway Fume Blanc

## Saute de Ris de Veau financiere
# Veal Sweetbreads Financiere

*Serves 4*

*This elegant dish consists of veal sweetbreads in Madeira sauce with mushrooms, olives, truffles, and veal quenelles. The original financiere garnishes also included the comb and kidneys of a cock—impossible to obtain commercially these days! Make the quenelles and blanch the sweetbreads ahead of time, and the final preparation of this dish will take very little time.*

*To prepare sweetbreads*

> 1 stalk celery
> 1 carrot
> 1 leek, white part only
> 1 onion, peeled
> Salt
> 4 bay leaves
> 4 whole cloves
> 10-15 black peppercorns
> 1 teaspoon pickling spice
> 2 pounds fresh veal sweetbreads

Wash celery, carrot, and leek; chop these and onion into large pieces. Place vegetables into a soup pot with two quarts of salted water and all seasonings. Boil for 10 to 15 minutes; then add sweetbreads and blanch for four to five minutes. Remove sweetbreads to cool. Discard water with vegetables. Clean sweetbreads by removing all skin and slice ¼ inch thick. Set aside.

*To prepare veal quenelles*

> ½ pound ground veal
> ¼ cup ice water

Salt
Freshly ground white pepper
Freshly ground or grated nutmeg
2 egg whites
½ cup heavy cream

Place ground veal and ice water into food processor; sprinkle with salt, pepper, and nutmeg. Blend at high speed until very fine. Then add egg whites and cream and mix again for about 20 seconds, or just until egg whites and cream are blended. Refrigerate for at least one hour.

In a shallow pan, bring lightly salted water to a simmer. Using a teaspoon, form little balls the shape and size of an unshelled almond and drop into the water. Repeat this until you have four to six pieces per person. Simmer for five to eight minutes. Keep warm in the water until needed.

*To prepare sauce*

¾ cup demi-glace (page 6)

8 pieces duck liver
Salt
Freshly ground black pepper
Flour
5 tablespoons butter
20 small button mushrooms
¼ cup Madeira wine
20 small pitted olives
4 slices truffle, optional

Season sweetbreads and duck liver with salt and pepper. Flour them very lightly and shake off any excess flour. Wash mushrooms and remove stems.

In a large skillet, heat three tablespoons of the butter. When butter is foaming, add sweetbreads and saute for two minutes on each side. Remove from pan and keep warm. Add mush-

*Meat and Game*    153

rooms to the skillet and saute for three or four more minutes. Add Madeira wine and deglaze. Stir in demi-glace and olives; let simmer.

While sauce is simmering, saute duck liver in another skillet for three or four minutes in one tablespoon of the butter. Remove from pan and keep warm.

Now whisk remaining butter into simmering sauce bit by bit. Gently add the veal quenelles to the sauce.

Arrange sweetbreads on individual plates decorated with 2 duck livers each. Spoon the sauce over the sweetbreads. Top with a slice of truffle if desired and serve.

*Suggested Wines*

> Freemark Abbey Cabernet Sauvignon
> Dry Creek Cabernet Sauvignon

## Meᴆᴀɪʟʟonꜱ ᴆᴇ Veᴀu Mᴀnᴆᴀʀɪn
## Veal Medallions Mandarin

*Serves 4*

*This veal dish with an oriental flavor is served with curried rice, mango chutney, and sauce maltaise, which is a hollandaise sauce made with tomato catsup and the juice of blood oranges. I prefer to use Major Grey's mango chutney for its superior flavor and texture.*

> ½ cup sauce maltaise (page 49)
> 2 cups cooked rice (page 193)
>
> 3 tablespoons oil
> ¾ cup flour
> 1 egg
> ¾ cup beer

Sugar
½ teaspoon salt
Freshly ground white pepper

1½ pounds trimmed veal tenderloin
6 tablespoons butter

1 banana, quartered
Oil for deep-frying

1 to 1½ tablespoons curry powder
24 orange segments
4 slices pineapple, ¼ inch thick
6 tablespoons mango chutney

## To prepare beer batter

Whisk oil and flour together in a bowl. Add egg, then slowly add beer, whisking constantly. Stir in a pinch of sugar, salt, and a sprinkling of freshly ground white pepper. Everything should be well blended; the batter should be very smooth. Set aside.

## To prepare veal

Slice tenderloin into 12 two-ounce medallions. Flatten these slightly with a mallet. Season with salt and freshly ground white pepper; flour very lightly.

Heat five tablespoons of the butter in a large skillet (or use two skillets and divide the butter) over medium to high heat. When butter is foaming, saute veal medallions for three to four minutes on each side, or until done to your liking. Remove veal from skillet and keep warm.

## To prepare bananas and serve

Dip banana pieces into beer batter and deep fry until golden brown. Drain on absorbent paper and keep warm.

Heat remaining butter in a skillet. Add curry powder and mix well. When butter starts to foam, add rice, mix thoroughly, and heat through. Season with salt.

Place curried rice on individual plates. Set three veal medallions on top of rice. Top each medallion with a spoonful of sauce maltaise and decorate with two orange segments. Garnish each plate with a fried banana quarter and a slice of pineapple. Serve with mango chutney on the side.

*Suggested Wines*

> Chateau St. Jean Johannisberg Riesling
> Grand Cru Chenin Blanc

## Cotelettes d'Agneau Grille Maison
## Grilled Lamb Chops
*Serves 4*

*This highly decorative and delectable lamb dish is a specialty of the Abbey. Each of the three trimmed and grilled lamb rib chops is placed on a crouton and topped with seasoned diced tomatoes. On one is placed an artichoke bottom with bearnaise sauce; on another a sauteed lamb kidney; and on the third a mushroom cap with fresh, shredded horseradish. (Note: Ask the butcher to "french" the rib chops, trimming the fat and gristle from the bone.)*

> 4 cooked artichoke bottoms (page 185)
> ¼ cup bearnaise sauce (page 45)
>
> 3 tablespoons butter
> 1 shallot, peeled and chopped fine
> 2 medium tomatoes, peeled and diced
> 1 garlic clove, minced
> Salt
> Freshly ground white pepper
> 4 large mushroom caps, washed and stems removed

Squeeze of lemon juice
12 lamb rib chops, 3-3½ ounces each
4 lamb kidneys
12 white bread rounds, 2 to 2½ inches
3 tablespoons grated fresh horseradish

Melt one tablespoon of the butter in each of two small skillets. Place chopped shallots in one skillet and saute until translucent. Add diced tomatoes and garlic; season with salt and pepper to taste. Saute for four to five minutes.

When butter is foaming in the other skillet, add mushroom caps. Sprinkle with salt, pepper, and lemon juice and saute for six to seven minutes or until mushrooms are done.

In a third skillet, melt the remaining tablespoon of butter. Heat cooked artichoke bottoms in the butter.

Clean kidneys well and split in half. Season lamb chops and kidneys on both sides with salt and pepper. Broil lamb chops for approximately four minutes on each side, actual cooking time depending on desired degree of doneness. When chops are about half done, place kidneys under broiler so that both will be ready at the same time. (If you do not have a broiler, saute the chops and kidneys in a little butter.)

Butter bread rounds on both sides and brown in a hot oven or under a broiler. Place three bread croutons in a line on each plate. Place a lamb chop on each crouton with the bones pointing away from the plate. Spoon some diced tomatoes on the first chop and top with two pieces of lamb kidney. Place an artichoke bottom, open side up, on the center chop, and fill it with bearnaise sauce. Spoon tomatoes on the third chop; top with a horseradish-filled mushroom cap.

*Suggested Wines*

Ridge Coast Zinfandel
Lytton Springs Winery Zinfandel

## Selle ò'agneau en feuilletage
## Saddle of Lamb in Puff Pastry

*Serves 4 to 6*

*This roast saddle of a whole lamb loin is boned and trimmed; filled with a mixture of spinach, duck liver, and mushrooms; and then baked in puff pastry. I serve it with a light lamb sauce, and with Berny potatoes, stuffed zucchini with eggplant and tomatoes, or cauliflower au gratin.*

1 recipe puff pastry dough (page 195)

⅓ cup fine-diced mushrooms
5 tablespoons butter
⅓ cup fine-diced duck liver
Salt
Freshly ground white pepper
1/8 cup fine-chopped uncooked bacon
2 shallots, chopped fine
½ pound spinach
Freshly ground or grated nutmeg
1 whole loin of lamb, deboned and trimmed, leaving 1/8"
   fat on top
1 egg
¼ cup light cream

In a skillet, saute mushrooms in one tablespoon of the butter for three to four minutes. Add duck liver seasoned with salt and pepper and saute over high heat until liver is seared but still pink inside, two to three minutes. Pour this mixture into a bowl.

Wash spinach and trim stems; blanch one to two minutes. Drain and chop.

Heat two tablespoons of the butter, add bacon and saute for three minutes. Then add shallots and cook for three more minutes. Add spinach; season with salt, pepper, and nutmeg; and saute for three to five minutes. Pour this mixture into the liver and mushrooms and mix well. Cool.

Spread the lamb lengthwise, fat side down, and flatten slightly with the flat side of a cleaver. Spread the spinach mixture on top, roll the lamb, and secure it with kitchen string, tied in crosswise rows about one inch apart. Then tie it twice lengthwise to contain the filling. Season stuffed loin with salt and pepper, and brown quickly in the remaining butter in a very hot skillet so the meat will be kept very rare. Remove from skillet and set aside to cool. Remove string.

Roll puff dough into a rectangle, then fold in thirds and roll again into a rectangle. Fold in thirds again, then roll out until 1/8 inch thick. Place the lamb on one end of the piece of dough. Fold the other end of the dough over the meat to enclose it completely, allowing an overlap of about an inch. Mix the egg with cream and brush the edges and the seams of the dough with this. Decorate the top with remaining dough, and brush this also with the egg wash.

Place lamb saddle seam side down in a shallow roasting pan. Roast in a preheated 475°F oven for about 20 minutes. Remove from oven and let sit for eight to ten minutes. Slice into 1 to 1½-inch thick pieces, arrange on individual serving plates, and serve.

*Suggested Wines*

Chateau Montelena Zinfandel
Buena Vista Zinfandel

noisettes ỏ'agneau au porto
## Lamb Tenderloin with Veal Sweetbreads
*Serves 4*

*To serve four people you will need eight tenderloins, so if you wish you can substitute the trimmed, boned lamb loin cut into medallions. These are sauteed with veal sweetbreads and lamb kidneys and then served with a port wine sauce. Prepare the sweetbreads first, according to the recipe on page 152.*

4 slices cooked veal sweetbreads, about ½ pound
(page 152)
⅓ cup demi-glace (page 6)
¼ cup creme fraiche (page 49)

1½ pound boneless trimmed lamb loin
5 tablespoons butter
4 lamb kidneys
⅓ cup vintage port
Salt
Freshly ground white pepper

Slice lamb loin into twelve equal pieces (noisettes), approximately two ounces each. Flatten each slightly and season with salt and pepper.

Clean kidneys well, cut in half, and season also.

Heat four tablespoons of the butter in a large skillet and saute noisettes for three to four minutes on each side. When noisettes are about half done, add kidneys and saute. Both will be ready at the same time. Lamb should be pink on the inside. Remove from skillet to a plate and keep warm.

Drain about half of the cooking fat. Deglaze pan with port wine and simmering, uncovered, reduce by about half. Meanwhile, in remaining butter in another skillet, saute the sweetbreads lightly, two to three minutes on each side. Keep sweetbreads warm with meat. Add demi-glace to reduced wine, bring to a boil, and simmer for four to five minutes.

On each serving plate, arrange three noisettes, two pieces lamb kidney, and one slice veal sweetbread.

Add any accumulated meat juices to the sauce. Add creme fraiche and stir well. Correct seasoning if necessary.

Spoon sauce over meat and serve immediately.

*Suggested Wines*

> Caymus Zinfandel
> Chappellet Cabernet Sauvignon

## Medaillons de porc Milanaise
## Pork Medallions Milanaise
*Serves 4*

*A Milanaise garnish traditionally includes ham, mushrooms, truffles, and tongue, served with spaghetti and a tomato sauce. The medallions of pork, breaded with crumbs and Parmesan cheese and sauteed, are complemented beautifully by this combination. I accompany the dish with a green salad vinaigrette or other crisp green vegetable.*

> 1 cup tomato sauce (page 41)
>
> ½ pound uncooked spaghetti
> 4 eggs
> ¼ cup light cream or milk
> 1½ pounds trimmed pork tenderloin
> Salt
> Freshly ground black pepper
> Flour

Fresh bread crumbs
Grated Parmesan cheese
10 tablespoons butter
½ cup sliced mushrooms
½ cup cooked julienne of ham
Julienne of truffles, optional
Freshly ground or grated nutmeg

Cook spaghetti in boiling salt water al dente, rinse in cold water, and set aside.

Slice the tenderloin into 12 two-ounce medallions and flatten each slightly.

Mix eggs with cream to make an egg wash. Season pork with salt and pepper, and flour very lightly. Shake off any excess flour. Mix bread crumbs with Parmesan cheese, measuring three times as much crumbs as cheese by volume. Dip medallions into egg wash and then into bread crumb mixture, pressing this dry mixture firmly onto the meat with your hands. Then shake off any excess.

In each of two large skillets heat four tablespoons of the butter. When butter is foaming, place six medallions into each pan and saute four to five minutes on each side. Both sides should be nicely browned. Remove from skillet and keep warm.

Heat remaining butter over medium heat, add mushrooms and saute for three to four minutes. Add julienned ham and truffles if desired. Saute three to four more minutes. Add cooked spaghetti, season with salt and nutmeg, mix well and saute until spaghetti is hot. Bring tomato sauce to a boil in a small saucepan. Arrange meat on a serving dish. Sprinkle each medallion with a little more Parmesan and brown quickly under a broiler. Serve tomato sauce and spaghetti on the side.

To serve this dish on individual plates, place sauce underneath the pork medallions and not on top. Otherwise, the meat would get soggy.

*Suggested Wines*

>Sterling Sauvignon Blanc
>Mondavi Gamay Rose

## Noisettes de Chevreuil Nouvelle Epoque
## Marinated Venison rounds
*Serves 4*

*Small morsels of venison are sliced from the loin or tenderloin, marinated for a full day, and sauteed with chanterelle mushrooms, then served with a green peppercorn sauce. We accompany this dish with braised stuffed apple and a mixed fresh fruit salad with a mayonnaise and whipped cream dressing. It is also good with homemade noodles, and red cabbage or Brussels sprouts.*

*To marinate meat*

>1½ pounds brimmed venison loin
>3 cups dry red wine
>2 onions, peeled and diced
>2 cups milk
>2 tablespoons juniper berries, crushed
>Bay leaves, 4 fresh or 3 dried
>6-8 crushed black peppercorns

Mix red wine, onions, milk, and seasonings. Pour this marinade over the whole loin in a bowl. Cover and refrigerate for 12 to 15 hours, turning occasionally.

*To prepare Salade Capri*

¼ pound seedless grapes, washed and halved
¼ cup mandarin or other orange segments, without
   membranes
¼ cup peeled, sliced apples
¼ cup diced pineapple
6-8 strawberries, washed and halved
1 teaspoon mayonnaise
1 tablespoon sugar
Juice from ½ lemon
¼ pint heavy cream
1 head Boston lettuce, washed
¼ cup shelled walnuts

Beat cream with a touch of sugar until stiff. Mix all fruit
together in a bowl with mayonnaise, add sugar and lemon
juice, and fold in whipped cream. Line individual dessert
plates with lettuce, top with fruit salad, and decorate with
walnuts. Refrigerate until ready to serve.

*To prepare braised apples*

4 small apples
¼ cup raisins
4 tablespoons red currant jelly
Ground cinnamon
1 cup sweet white wine
Juice from 1 lemon
6 tablespoons sugar

Peel apples and trim into a nicely rounded shape. Core apples,
leaving a thin "floor," and fill with raisins. Top each with one
tablespoon red currant jelly and sprinkle with cinnamon
powder.

Place into a shallow baking pan containing one cup of white
wine and juice from one lemon; sprinkle sugar on top of apples. Bake in a preheated 375°F oven until done, about 15
minutes. Keep warm.

*To prepare meat and sauce*

1 cup venison green peppercorn sauce (page 31)

Flour
6 tablespoons butter
2 tablespoons cognac
1 shallot, chopped fine
Chanterelle mushrooms, ¾ cup canned or ½ pound fresh
Salt
Freshly ground black pepper
Marinated venison loin

Place venison loin on cutting board, dry off remaining marinade with paper towels, and slice into 12 equal pieces (noisettes), approximately two ounces each. Flatten each noisette slightly; season with salt and pepper.

Lightly dust noisettes with flour, shaking off any excess. Heat four tablespoons of the butter in a large skillet over medium to high heat. When butter is foaming, saute noisettes for two to four minutes on each side. Noisettes should remain pink inside. Remove noisettes from pan and keep warm. Deglaze pan with cognac. Pour in venison pepper sauce and simmer.

In another skillet, saute shallots in remaining butter until translucent. Add chanterelles, sprinkle with salt and pepper, and saute for four or five minutes. Pour contents of this skillet into the sauce and mix well.

Place three noisettes on each individual serving plate. Top with several spoonfuls of sauce. Place a baked apple on each plate and serve immediately with Salade Capri on the side.

*Suggested Wines*

Calera Wine Company Zinfandel
Freemark Abbey Cabernet Sauvignon

## Selle ᴅᴇ Lievre Roti a la Creme
# Roast Saddle of Hare in Cream Sauce

*Serves 4 to 6*

*Look for a young, tender hare of about a year, and use the saddle of the animal; or purchase domestic rabbit and prepare the dish from the tenderest loin and rib parts. If you choose to use the legs as well, note that legs must roast a little longer than the saddle, so they should be split apart and the saddle removed first. You will need a needle to lard the hare (available in a gourmet shop). Serve with Berny potatoes or potato croquettes, and Brussels sprouts or red cabbage. Any kind of wild mushrooms makes a wonderful accompaniment.*

½ cup demi-glace (page 6)
¼ cup beef stock (page 4)
½ cup creme fraiche (page 49)

½ to ¾ pound fatback
3 whole saddles of hare, bone-in and trimmed
Salt
Freshly ground black pepper
4 tablespoons butter
1 carrot
1 stalk celery
1 onion, peeled
2 bay leaves
4-5 cloves
¼ cup dry red wine
Juice from ½ lemon

Cut fatback into strips, 1½ inches long and 1/8 inch thick. Using a larding needle, "stitch" strips of pork fat across the width of the saddles. (For details, see page 139.) Season with salt and pepper.

Wash carrot and celery; chop these and onion into large pieces.

Melt butter in a roasting pan. Place saddle, meaty side down, in pan and arrange chopped vegetables around it. Add bay leaves and cloves. Roast in 325°F oven, turning saddle and basting occasionally, for approximately 25 minutes. Saddle should be slightly pink inside. Remove saddle from pan and keep warm.

Pour demi-glace, beef stock, and red wine into pan and simmer for approximately 20 minutes. Add creme fraiche and simmer for five more minutes. Strain sauce, then return to heat. Bring to a boil; add lemon juice and season with salt and pepper.

Remove saddle meat from bone and slice ¼ inch thick. Serve with sauce on the side.

*Suggested Wines*

Sterling Merlot
Rutherford Hill Merlot

# Vegetables and Side Dishes

HE VEGETABLES AND SIDE DISHES served with a fine gourmet meal can do more than anything to enhance the pleasure of an elegant entree; their preparation need not be time-consuming, but it must be carefully considered. At the Abbey we serve three different vegetables with each entree, as well as a potato dish. We are careful not to repeat in the side dish a vegetable that is already present in another form in the entree; and, of course, some entrees such as Nasi Goreng are prepared with so many vegetables that no additional dishes need accompany them.

Certain dishes go so well with particular vegetables that they are always served in tandem—roast goose, for example, with red cabbage; or venison with chanterelle mushrooms; or beef Frascati with a stuffed mushroom cap and asparagus. But the old traditions of serving lamb with the inevitable green beans, for instance, are no longer strict rules; and it can be part of the pleasure of preparing a meal to create an imaginative complement to a classic entree. We serve quite a few stuffed vegetables at the Abbey, and the variations possible in stuffing ingredients offer almost limitless opportunities to the experimental chef.

Several recipes presented in this chapter do not specify amounts for the vegetables you will be using, or the number of servings to be produced. In these cases, your own judgment will easily suffice, as seasonings are merely added to taste. The cardinal rule of cooking vegetables, of course, is to start with the freshest possible produce. I comb the farmers' market for firm, unflawed, green vegetables and vine-ripened tomatoes; and I accept any offer of a fresh home-grown product. When slightly undercooked to retain a crisp bite, and delicately seasoned, the humble vegetable can rank with the most complicated recipe as fit for any discriminating palate.

## ᴀꜱᴘᴇʀɢᴇꜱ
# White Asparagus with Brown Butter
*Serves 4*

*Perhaps because of my German background I prefer the white asparagus that is customary on the continent to the green asparagus with its more distinctive flavor, which is more common in America. Fresh white asparagus from California is available now; remember to peel away the outer membrane on the stalk and cook it until it is soft. Green can also be peeled, but I prefer not to do so; and it is better a little undercooked, so that it still has a crisp texture. I have included a recipe for each type of asparagus; but the browned butter method works well for both, and any number of sauces combine well with either.*

> 2 pounds white asparagus
> Salt
> Touch of sugar
> 3 tablespoons butter

Using a potato peeler, peel asparagus from the head down. Trim approximately 1½ inches from the bottom of each piece. Divide asparagus into four servings, approximately a half pound each. Hold each serving in your hand to form a bunch and tie with a string to hold together.

Bring a half gallon of salted water to boil; add a touch of sugar. Immerse asparagus and boil for about 20 minutes or until tender. Remove asparagus to a serving plate; keep warm.

In a skillet, melt butter until foaming; then carefully cook butter for approximately a minute more, or until butter has nut brown color. Do not burn. Pour brown butter over asparagus and serve.

**Green Asparagus.** Cook the same way as for white asparagus, but reduce cooking time so asparagus will be still crunchy. When finished cooking, plunge into ice water immediately to keep green color. When ready to serve, reheat in a bit of water and a little butter. Serve with hollandaise sauce, page 48.

## Les Broccolis a la polonaise
## Broccoli a la Polonaise

*Serves 6 to 8*

*I never saw broccoli until 1960, when I was introduced to it as "Italian asparagus" in the course of my training as a chef! Now it is the basis for many Abbey vegetable dishes, whether in timbales or a souffle, or covered with a polonaise sauce. Polish in origin, the same sauce can be used with equal success over asparagus or cauliflower.*

Broccoli, enough for 6-8 servings
½ pound butter
1 hard-cooked egg, chopped
½ tablespoon chopped fresh parsley
2 tablespoons bread crumbs
Salt
Freshly ground white pepper

Cook broccoli in boiling salt water for approximately 15 minutes. Do not overcook—keep crisp. Then plunge into ice water to cool. Trim the ends and place broccoli into a baking dish.

Melt butter in a saucepan. Add egg, parsley, and bread crumbs. Simmer for several minutes. Season with salt and pepper. Spoon sauce over broccoli. Bake in a 350°F oven for about five minutes. Then broil to brown sauce lightly.

## Choux de Bruxelles
## Brussels Sprouts
*Serves any number*

*This is my favorite simple recipe for Brussels sprouts. Adapt the amounts of ingredients depending on the number of people you want to serve.*

Brussels sprouts
Onion, chopped fine
Raw bacon, optional, chopped fine
Butter
Salt
Freshly ground white pepper
Freshly ground or grated nutmeg

Cut the ends from the Brussels sprouts and remove the outer leaves. Rinse well and cook in boiling salted water for 10 to 15 minutes. Then plunge immediately into ice water to cool and maintain the green color. Drain well.

Saute onions (and bacon if desired) in butter for three to four minutes; then add Brussels sprouts. Season with salt, pepper, and nutmeg. Saute for three to four minutes more; then serve.


## Chou Rouge
## Red Cabbage
*Serves 4 to 6*

*A spicy, redolent, dark red dish with a German flavor. The cabbage is marinated for several hours, and then braised with a little leftover goose or bacon fat, apples, and onions. Pungent and delicious!*

1 cup beef stock (page 4) or water

1 head red cabbage
Red wine vinegar
Salt
Sugar

3 tablespoons bacon fat
2 onions, peeled and sliced
2 apples, peeled and sliced
½ cup red wine
½ cinnamon stick
5-6 cloves
Freshly ground white pepper
2 bay leaves

Remove outer leaf from cabbage head; quarter and remove core. Shred cabbage finely, by hand or with a blender or food processor. Marinate for several hours in a little red wine vinegar seasoned with salt and sugar. Drain, saving a small amount of marinade.

Heat bacon fat in a large, non-aluminum pot. Add onion and apple slices and cook over medium heat for two to three minutes. Add drained, marinated cabbage and mix well. Stir in beef stock, red wine, cinnamon, cloves, pepper, bay leaves, and a touch of the marinade.

Simmer gently for an hour, stirring frequently. Add a touch of red wine vinegar, salt, and sugar and cook for five to eight more minutes. By this time, liquid should be reduced to a small amount, but you also could thicken it slightly by adding a raw shredded potato or a touch of cornstarch (mixed first with a little cold water or red wine) and simmering a few more minutes.

# Choucroute au Vin de Champagne
## Champagne Sauerkraut

*Serves 4*

*Juniper berries and champagne give this dish a wonderful combination of sweet and tart flavors. I buy the best quality German sauerkraut, either Gundelsheim or Hengstenberg; if the taste of the sauerkraut you obtain is very vinegary, you might want to rinse it before preparing this dish. The addition of fresh diced pineapple makes a delicious variation on this recipe.*

1 cup beef stock (page 4)

2-3 tablespoons bacon fat
1-2 onions, peeled and sliced
1 16-ounce can sauerkraut
Sugar
Salt
Freshly ground white pepper
2 bay leaves
3-5 juniper berries
½ to 1 cup champagne

Heat pork fat in a non-aluminum pot. Add onions and saute for three to four minutes. Add sauerkraut; season with sugar, salt, and pepper. Stir in stock, bay leaves, and juniper berries. Simmer for 1 to 1½ hours, stirring frequently. Liquid should be very much reduced by this time. Thicken slightly by adding a shredded raw potato or a touch of cornstarch (mixed first with a little cold water or champagne) and simmering a few more minutes. Add champagne, bring to a quick boil, and serve.

**Champagne Sauerkraut with Pineapple.** Prepare as above, adding ¾ cup diced fresh pineapple with the champagne.

## Carottes Glacees
# Glazed Carrots

*Serves any number*

*Carrots should always be undercooked slightly, to retain their crispness and "bite."*

    Shallots, chopped fine
    Butter
    Baby carrots
    Salt
    Sugar

Saute shallots in butter until tender. Add peeled and washed carrots, salt, sugar, and a touch of water. Braise over medium heat until juice is totally reduced and carrots have a shiny glaze. Do not overcook carrots; they should be firm and a little crunchy.

## Oignons Glaces
# Glazed Pearl Onions

*Serves any number*

*Peeled, blanched, and glazed, these serve less as a vegetable than as a garnish with meat dishes and stews.*

    Pearl onions, peeled
    Butter
    Sugar
    Salt

Boil onions for five to eight minutes in salted water. Cool and drain well. Heat butter in a skillet until it is a very light brown color. Add a little sugar; then add onions and mix until well coated. Season with salt and saute for four to five minutes.

## haricots verts
# Green Beans with Bacon

*Serves any number*

*The true haricot vert is a small, thin French bean, probably the finest bean to be had, and delicious when simply sauteed with shallots and butter. It is possible to obtain them from California, but when I must use fresh green snap beans instead, I prepare them with bacon as in this recipe.*

> Green beans
> Raw bacon strips
> Melted butter
> Salt
> Freshly ground white pepper

Cut ends from stringbeans and boil in salted water for 12 to 15 minutes, or until done but still crisp. Drain and cool in ice water.

Place a half bacon strip on a flat surface. Lay eight to ten beans across the bacon and roll the bacon around them. Trim beans to equal lengths on either side of bacon.

Place beans in a shallow baking dish with a touch of water and a drizzle of melted butter. Season with salt and freshly ground white pepper. Bake in a preheated 350°F oven for five to eight minutes. Then broil briefly to crisp bacon.

# Champignons farcis
# Stuffed Mushrooms

*Serves 6*

*You can stuff mushrooms with almost anything you want to,
which is one reason that they are such an endlessly versatile
vegetable side dish. Here is one recipe I use more often at the
Abbey.*

1 tablespoon beef or chicken stock (pages 4, 8)

6 large fresh mushrooms, washed, stems removed
Salt
Freshly ground white pepper
Touch lemon juice
2 tablespoons butter
1 bacon strip, chopped fine
½ onion, peeled and chopped fine
1 peeled tomato, seeds removed and diced fine
½ garlic clove, minced
1 tablespoon fresh bread crumbs
½ tablespoon chopped fresh parsley

Season mushroom caps with salt, pepper, and a squeeze of
lemon juice. Saute in a half tablespoon of the butter for three
to four minutes. Arrange mushrooms in baking dish, open side
up.

In a half tablespoon of the butter, saute bacon for three to four
minutes. Add onions and cook for three more minutes. Then
add tomatoes, garlic, and another touch of lemon juice.
Season with salt and freshly ground white pepper. Cook this
for three to four minutes. Add bread crumbs and chopped
parsley, mix well and moisten with beef or chicken stock.

Stuff each mushroom cap. Melt remaining butter and pour
over stuffed mushrooms. Bake in preheated 400°F oven for six
to eight minutes.

*Vegetables and Side Dishes* 177

## Chanterelles au Lardi
## Wild Mushrooms with Bacon
*Serves 4 to 6*

*I think that the chanterelle mushroom from the woods of France and Germany is one of the finest to be had; and at the Abbey we fly chanterelles in from Europe whenever they are in season. They have a wonderful, subtly woody flavor that makes an excellent complement to the onions, bacon, and fresh herbs in this dish.*

    2 strips bacon, chopped fine
    1 ½ tablespoons butter
    1 onion, chopped fine
    1 pound chanterelles, cleaned and washed
    Salt
    Freshly ground white pepper
    Chopped fresh parsley

Saute bacon in the butter until translucent. Add onion and saute for three more minutes. Add chanterelles, reduce heat, and cook gently for 10 to 15 minutes. Season with salt and pepper, sprinkle with chopped parsley, and serve.

# Cepes a la Provencale
## Stone Mushrooms with Tomatoes and Garlic
*Serves 4 to 6*

*When I was a child in Germany we used to go out at four or five in the morning to pick wild mushrooms in the dewy dawn. Cepes can be purchased dried and then soaked in water an hour or so before you use them, and they are also available in cans, though I find this less satisfactory. This side dish uses tomato and garlic to accent the lovely, delicate flavor of the cepes, or stone mushrooms.*

> 5-6 ounces dried stone mushrooms (cepes)
> 1 small shallot, chopped fine
> Salad oil
> Salt
> Freshly ground pepper
> 1 medium tomato, peeled and diced
> 1 clove garlic, minced
> Chopped parsley

Soak dried cepes in cold water for one hour, drain well, and dry.

Saute chopped shallots in oil until translucent. Add cepes and saute for two to three minutes. Season with salt and pepper. Add tomatoes and garlic. Cook for three to four more minutes. Sprinkle with chopped parsley and serve.

## Epinaròs en Branches
# Sauteed Leaf Spinach

*Serves any number*

*The basic seasonings to use for spinach are salt, pepper, and freshly ground or grated nutmeg. It helps to wash, trim, and blanch the spinach ahead of time, and keep it in ice water until ready to use. Sauteed spinach can also be made without prior blanching.*

> Fresh spinach
> Shallots
> Butter
> Salt
> Freshly ground white pepper
> Freshly ground or grated nutmeg

Blanch well-washed leaf spinach in boiling water for a minute or two. Plunge into ice water and drain well.

Saute chopped shallots in butter until translucent; then add spinach. Season with salt, freshly ground white pepper, and freshly ground nutmeg. Saute for a minute more. Serve hot.

## Epinaròs à la Creme
# Creamed Spinach

*Serves 4*

*This creamed spinach is a simple but delightful dish; blanch the spinach ahead of time, and remember to season it well to offset the flavor of the cream. It is good made with broccoli as well, although the bacon should be omitted in that case.*

> 1 pound spinach, well washed, stems removed

2 tablespoons butter
2 strips bacon, chopped fine
1-2 peeled shallots, chopped fine
½ tablespoon flour
⅓ cup heavy cream
Salt
Freshly ground white pepper
Freshly ground nutmeg
½ garlic clove, minced

Blanch spinach in salted water for three to four minutes; then plunge into ice water to keep the bright green color. After cooling, squeeze all water out of spinach and then mince fine, either by hand or with a food processor or blender.

Melt butter in a medium saucepan, add bacon, and saute for three to four minutes. Add shallots and cook over medium heat for three more minutes. Then add flour, mix well, add cream, and stir again. Bring to a boil, then add spinach. Reduce heat to simmer. Season with salt, pepper, nutmeg, and garlic. Simmer for three to four more minutes, stirring constantly. Serve at once.

**Creamed Broccoli.** Prepare as for creamed spinach, substituting one pound of broccoli for the spinach and omitting the bacon. The broccoli needs to be cooked longer initially, about 15 minutes instead of three to four; trim the woody stems from the cooked broccoli before mincing.

## Spinach Timbales

*Serves 6 to 8*

*Use the creamed spinach puree from the preceding recipe to make this lovely vegetable side dish; and remember to season the mixture strongly, as the egg whites and the cream will dilute the flavors. One can cook a timbale in a large dish rather than individual dishes, but it will need to cook longer before it is done. A broccoli variation follows the recipe.*

1½ pounds cooked creamed spinach (page 180)

Melted butter
2 egg yolks, lightly beaten
2-3 egg whites, whipped until stiff

Thoroughly butter six to eight ramekin dishes (4-ounce size) and set aside.

To the cooled creamed spinach, add egg yolks and mix well. Fold in egg whites so they are completely incorporated.

Place ramekins in a baking pan approximately 2½ inches deep. Spoon mixture into ramekins. Knock the pan gently on a table to settle the mixture. Add approximately two inches of hot water to the pan.

Bake in a preheated 275-300° oven for 40 to 45 minutes.

Remove ramekins from baking pan; then loosen the edges of the timbales by running a sharp knife around the edge of each. Unmold onto a serving dish.

**Broccoli Timbales.** Prepare as for spinach timbales, substituting 1½ pounds creamed broccoli for the creamed spinach.

# Creamed Yellow Squash

*Serves 8*

*This abundant summer vegetable adapts well to a light, creamy preparation. Unlike other creamed vegetables, the squash should retain a slight crispness.*

2 bacon strips, chopped fine
2 tablespoons butter
1 onion, chopped fine
3-4 medium yellow squash, washed and thin sliced
3 scallions, chopped fine
1 garlic clove, minced
Salt
Freshly ground white pepper
1 teaspoon flour
⅓ cup heavy cream
½ tablespoon chopped parsley

Saute bacon in butter over medium heat for three to four minutes. Add onion and cook for three more minutes. Then stir in sliced squash, green onions, and garlic. Season with salt and pepper. Continue cooking over low to medium heat for about 10 minutes, or until squash is almost cooked through, but not soft.

Sprinkle with flour and mix well. Add cream, mix again, and simmer for three to four minutes. Sprinkle with chopped parsley and serve.

CONCOMBRES à la CRÈME
## Cucumbers in Cream
*Serves any number*

*This is an unusual way to serve this plentiful summer vegetable.*

    Cucumbers
    Butter
    Salt
    Freshly ground white pepper
    Heavy cream

Slice peeled cucumbers into 1½ to 2 inch long pieces, then cut in half lengthwise, or into quarters if cucumber is very thick. Remove seeds. Saute cucumbers in a little butter. Season with salt and pepper, then add heavy cream to cover the bottom of pan. Braise until done, 8 to 10 minutes.

CONCOMBRES FARCIS
## Stuffed Cucumbers
*Serves any number*

*People are not used to seeing cucumber as a hot vegetable, but it is a delicious one. I use the same stuffing as for veal quenelles.*

    Veal quenelles (page 152), uncooked
    Demi-glace (page 6)

    Cucumbers
    Salt
    Pepper

Peel cucumber, then slice into 1½-inch pieces. Stand pieces of cucumbers on end and scoop out the center, going halfway down. Season inside with salt and pepper; then stuff with veal mixture used for quenelles.

Set into a shallow pan with a little melted butter and nap with demi-glace. Bake at 325°F for 15 to 18 minutes, or until done.

## fonds d'artichauts farcis
## Stuffed Artichoke Bottoms
*Serves 6*

*This vegetable side dish takes very little time to prepare if one trims and boils the artichoke bottoms ahead of time. It can be varied with a number of bread stuffings, or vegetable fillings such as creamed spinach, ratatouille, or stewed tomatoes; this one is a delicious mushroom duxelle.*

Touch of demi-glace (page 6)

6 artichokes
2 lemons
Salt
1-2 tablespoons butter
1 shallot, chopped fine
¾ to 1 pound mushrooms, chopped fine
⅓ to ½ cup fine-chopped cooked ham
1 clove garlic, minced
Freshly ground white pepper
½ tablespoon chopped parsley
Parmesan cheese, grated
Bread crumbs

*To prepare artichokes*

Slice off top of artichoke, leaving only the lower section without leaves. Remove stem and scoop out hairy choke. Dip in lemon water or sprinkle with lemon juice to prevent browning.

Immerse in boiling, salted water flavored with the juice of one or two lemons. Boil 15 to 20 minutes. Remove from cooking liquid to cool. Allow liquid to cool also; then use it to store the cooked artichoke bottoms (to retain their color and flavor).

Just before stuffing, saute lightly in a small amount of butter.

*To prepare stuffing (mushroom duxelle)*

Saute shallots in butter for three to four minutes, or until translucent. Add mushrooms, ham, and garlic; season with salt and pepper and continue cooking for four to five minutes. Add demi-glace and cook eight to ten minutes more, or until reduced and duxelle has thickened. Add parsley.

*To serve*

Stuff cooked artichoke bottoms with mushroom duxelle. Sprinkle with Parmesan cheese and bread crumbs. Top each with bits of butter and bake in a preheated 375°F oven for five to seven minutes. Then brown lightly under a broiler and serve at once.

## Courgettes farcies
## Zucchini Stuffed with Tomatoes and Eggplant
*Serves 4 to 6*

*I slice thick slices of a young zucchini and stuff the slices individually for separate servings—more attractive and less unwieldy than a whole stuffed zucchini might be.*

¼ cup beef stock (page 4)

1 shallot, peeled and chopped fine
1 tablespoon olive oil
1 tablespoon butter

1 medium eggplant
Salt
Freshly ground white pepper
Sprig fresh oregano
1 clove garlic, minced
2 tomatoes, peeled and diced
1 tablespoon tomato paste
Grated Parmesan cheese
2 medium-to-large zucchini
Melted butter

Saute shallots in olive oil and butter for about two minutes, until tender but not browned.

Peel eggplant and dice into ¼-inch cubes; add to shallots and saute for four to five minutes. Add oregano and garlic; season with salt and pepper. Stir in diced tomatoes and tomato paste. Cook over medium heat for two to three minutes more; add beef stock and braise three to four more minutes. Allow to cool.

Wash zucchini well and trim both ends; slice into 1½-to-2 inch pieces. Stand pieces on end and scoop out the center, 1 to 1½ inches deep. Place in a shallow pan, season with salt and pepper, and drizzle with melted butter. Add just enough water to cover the bottom of the pan. Bake in a very slow (250°F) oven for 30 minutes or until almost cooked through.

Fill cooked zucchini centers with the vegetable stuffing. Sprinkle with Parmesan cheese, set into buttered pan, and bake at 350°F for five to eight minutes. Serve hot.

## tomates farcies
# Baked Stuffed Tomatoes

*Serves 6*

*For stuffing, it is best to look for smaller, firm tomatoes that will hold their shape well.*

4 tablespoons butter
½ onion, peeled
2 scallions, chopped fine
Sprig fresh basil
½ tablespoon chopped fresh chervil
½ tablespoon chopped parsley
½ tablespoon chopped fresh chives
½ cup bread crumbs
¼ cup Parmesan cheese
Salt
Freshly ground white pepper
1 garlic clove, minced
6 medium tomatoes, ripe but firm

Melt butter in a skillet, add onion, and saute for three to four minutes. Then add scallions, herbs, bread crumbs, and cheese; season with salt, pepper, and garlic. Mix thoroughly and set aside. If stuffing is too thick, add a touch of beef stock.

Cut out the hard core from the tomatoes, then turn tomatoes over. With a sharp knife, scoop out about a third of the tomato. Season this opening with salt and freshly ground white pepper. Spoon stuffing into each tomato. Place on baking sheet, sprinkle with oil, and bake at 350°F until tomato is done, about 12 to 15 minutes. Then broil until stuffing is lightly browned.

# Sauteed Cherry tomatoes

*Serves any number*

*The skin slips off cherry tomatoes most easily upon dipping them in hot oil, though boiling water will also do the job if you are careful to dip them for a few seconds only. They are delectable when sauteed in butter and seasoned with salt and pepper.*

> Large cherry tomatoes, ripe but firm
> Butter
> Salt
> Freshly ground white pepper

Briefly immerse tomatoes in a 375°F deep fryer, not long enough to break the skin (about 15 seconds). Cool tomatoes, then peel. Heat a little butter in a skillet. When butter is foaming, add tomatoes, but not too many at a time or they will get soft and break. Sprinkle with salt and freshly ground pepper and saute for two to three minutes.

# Baked Ratatouille

*Serves 4 to 6*

*A simple, colorful harvest casserole.*

> Touch of beef stock (page 4), optional
>
> 2 tomatoes, peeled
> 1 medium green pepper
> 1 small zucchini
> 1 medium eggplant
> 1½ medium onions, chopped fine
> 4 tablespoons olive oil
> Sprig of thyme
> 3 bay leaves

2 garlic cloves, minced
Salt
Freshly ground white pepper
1 tablespoon tomato paste
3 tablespoons Parmesan cheese

Remove seeds from tomatoes and dice. Dice green pepper, zucchini, and eggplant into ¼-inch cubes.

Saute onions in olive oil. Add green pepper, zucchini, and eggplant. Cook over medium heat for about 10 minutes, stirring frequently. Add all seasonings and herbs. Mix in diced tomatoes and tomato paste. Mix well and braise for four to five more minutes. If mixture is too thick, add a touch of beef stock or water. Place into casserole, sprinkle with Parmesan cheese and bake at 375°F for 10 to 15 minutes.

## pommes de terre parisienne
## Parisian Potatoes
*Serves any number*

*Use a melon ball cutter to shape the potatoes before they are sauteed with butter and parsley.*

Baking potatoes
Butter
Chopped fresh parsley

Peel potatoes. Then, with a small melon scoop, form potato balls. Cook in boiling, salted water until almost done, cool, and drain well.

Saute potatoes in a little butter until done and lightly browned all over. Sprinkle with salt and chopped parsley.

# pommes de terre Berny
## Berny Potatoes

*Serves 6*

*These potato croquettes are seasoned with chopped truffles and ham, formed into an apricot shape, then rolled in chopped almonds and deep fried.*

> 6 medium peeled baking potatoes
> ⅓ to ½ cup fine-chopped ham
> 1-2 truffles, chopped fine
> 6 egg yolks
> Salt
> Freshly ground white pepper
> Freshly ground or grated nutmeg
> Flour
> Egg wash (egg mixed with a little milk or cream)
> Almonds, chopped fine
> Oil for frying

Boil potatoes in salted water or steam until done. Drain well and dry by placing in a warm oven for a few minutes.

Press potatoes through a strainer or food mill or mash in a mixing bowl with a fork until very fine. Add ham, truffles, and egg yolks. Season with salt, pepper, and nutmeg. Mix well; then form potatoes into the shape of an apricot. Roll in flour, dip in egg wash, and cover with chopped almonds. Fry at 375°F until golden brown.

## nouilles fraiches
## Fresh Homemade Noodles
*Serves 4 to 6*

*This is a German noodle like spaetzle, made with a soft dough that I push through a colander into boiling water.*

2 cups flour
¼ cup olive oil
7 medium eggs
Salt
Freshly ground white pepper
Freshly ground or grated nutmeg

Measure flour into bowl. Whisk in olive oil and eggs, blending thoroughly until you have a smooth batter. Season with salt, pepper, and nutmeg.

Bring two quarts of salted water to a boil and set a colander on top of boiling water. Pour mixture into colander and, with a rubber spatula, press the batter through the colander into the water. With a spoon, stir water a little so noodles will not stick together. Boil for two to three minutes; then remove from pot, rinse under cold water, and drain well.

To store noddles in refrigerator, mix with a touch of oil and cover well.

To serve, melt one tablespoon of butter in a pan; add noodles, season with salt, pepper, and nutmeg, and heat for four to five minutes, stirring frequently.

RISOTTO AU SAFRAN
## Saffron Rice
*Serves 8*

*The basic rice served at the Abbey, this is flavored with mushrooms and green onions or shallots, garlic, and saffron, with a touch of lemon.*

4 cups beef or chicken stock (pages 4–5, 8)

1½ to 2 tablespoons butter
1 medium onion, chopped fine
3 scallions, chopped fine
2 cups white long-grain rice
Salt
Freshly ground white pepper
Juice from ½ lemon
2 pinches saffron

In an ovenproof pan large enough to cook the rice, melt butter and saute the onion and scallion for three to four minutes or until translucent. Add rice, salt, and pepper. Mix well so that all grains are coated with butter. Stir in stock, lemon juice and saffron. Cover, bake in 350°F oven for about 45 minutes or until rice has absorbed the liquid and has a firm texture.

# pastries
# and desserts

UY MOUGEL, the Abbey's pastry chef, came from France to America in 1959 after apprenticeship to a pastry chef near his home in Alsace-Lorraine. Since 1976 he has been at the Abbey, arriving well before dawn every day to begin making the cakes and confections that will grace the long dessert table at the dinner hour. We present here several of the best, for which we often receive recipe requests.

One happy fact about a delicious dessert is that it need not take much time or effort to prepare. Several of the recipes in this chapter—Orange Seville, Bananas Nourries, Strawberries Roman-off, and Crepes Fitzgerald are a few—are relatively simple, and at least as satisfying as a more elaborate preparation. The frozen Grand Marnier souffle is both elegant and impressive, a chilled bit of elegance that melts in the mouth. And if the labors of preparing the rest of your dinner have left you too limp to consider making a dessert at all, remember that fresh fruit in season, served with a compatible liqueur, will never disappoint your guests.

# puff pastry

*Yields 1 sheet pan dough, about 4 pounds*

*The Abbey's pastry chef, Guy Mougel, recommends adding a small amount of flour to the softened butter that will be spread on the pastry dough; the flour absorbs the water in the butter and makes it easier to roll. A wide variety of useful and decorative shapes—half-moons, rounds, and the like—can be cut from this basic puff pastry dough and baked in a hot oven until golden brown.*

½ teaspoon cream of tartar
5 cups all-purpose flour
1 cup plus 3 tablespoons cake flour
½ cup butter
1 jumbo egg (or 2 small)
1½ cups cold water
¼ teaspoon salt
1¼ pounds butter, softened and mixed with 4 tablespoons flour

Sift cream of tartar, all-purpose flour, and cake flour together. In a bowl, cut the half of butter into the dry ingredients until the mixture is very fine-grained with no discernible lumps.

Combine the egg, cold water, and salt and beat slightly. Add the egg mixture to the flour mixture and beat on medium speed for approximately five minutes to form a smooth dough.

Mold the dough into an oblong shape, cover with a damp cloth, and refrigerate for 30 minutes.

Place dough on pastry board or a cold flat surface and roll out into a rectangular shape. Cover two thirds of the dough with the softened butter-flour mixture. Fold the third of the dough that has not been covered with butter-flour over half of the covered dough; then fold the remaining portion over on top.

*Pastries and Desserts*   195

Turn the piece of dough sideways and roll out into rectangular shape approximately the same size as it was rolled into originally.

Fold in thirds again and reroll to same size rectangle. Then refrigerate for 30 minutes.

Remove dough from refrigerator and repeat folding in thirds and rolling back to original size two more times. Then rest dough in refrigerator for 24 hours.

When ready to use, remove from refrigerator only that amount of dough needed for immediate production. The rest will keep for four to eight days.

## plain Crepe Batter

*Yield: 3 dozen crepes*

*This is the basic crepe batter used for scallop brochettes and other crepe appetizers. Adding a little parsley to the batter gives it a nice flavor and appearance.*

4 medium eggs
¼ teaspoon salt
¼ teaspoon sugar
1½ cups flour
4 tablespoons vegetable oil
1 cup half-and-half
Chopped parsley

Mix eggs, salt, sugar, and flour until smooth, using a mixer, blender, or wire whip; slowly add oil and half-and-half and combine well. Let rest in refrigerator for at least an hour. Just before cooking, stir again.

Melt a tablespoon of butter in a crepe pan, and then wipe out the pan with a paper towel, so that only a thin coating remains. With a small ladle, pour two tablespoons of batter into hot pan, tilting pan so that batter covers the bottom. After a few seconds the crepe will be browned on one side; lift it with fingers or a fork and turn to brown quickly on the other side. Stack crepes to one side until batter is used up, wiping out pan occasionally with buttered paper towel.

## Strawberries Romanoff

*Serves 6*

*A simple but elegant dessert that is almost no trouble to prepare.*

> 1 quart fresh strawberries
> ½ cup Grand Marnier
> 4 tablespoons sugar
> 2 orange rinds, grated
> 2 tablespoons melba sauce (commercially available)
> 2 cups heavy cream, lightly sweetened and whipped stiff
> 4 scoops vanilla ice cream, softened

Wash strawberries and remove stems. Place in bowl and add Grand Marnier, sugar, orange rind, and melba sauce. Toss a few minutes to blend, and cover with a plate. Chill in refrigerator for one hour.

Remove strawberries from refrigerator, add whipped cream and mix. Add ice cream and stir just enough to blend all ingredients.

Divide mixture into individual sherbet glasses or dessert dishes. Serve immediately.

## CRepes fitzGeRald

*Yield: 2 dozen crepes*

*An elegant dessert crepe filled with a creamy mixture and served chilled, with a strawberry topping.*

*Batter*

 2 cups flour
 6 tablespoons sugar
 6 eggs
 4 tablespoons melted butter
 2 tablespoons Curacao liqueur
 2 cups milk

Mix flour, sugar, and eggs well using a mixer, blender, or wire whip. Add melted butter, liqueur, and milk and blend thoroughly. Rest in refrigerator for at least one hour. Just before making the crepes, stir again, as flour may have risen to the top.

*Filling*

 2 cups softened cream cheese
 1 cup sour cream
 ½ cup sugar
 1½ teaspoons vanilla

Beat cream cheese until smooth. Add sour cream, sugar, and vanilla and blend thoroughly.

Fill each crepe with two tablespoons cream cheese mixture and roll up. Sprinkle with powdered sugar and chill until ready to serve.

*Strawberry Topping*

 Fresh or frozen sliced strawberries

Sugar to taste
¼ cup maraschino liqueur or Grand Marnier

Combine all the ingredients in a saucepan. Bring to a boil; then simmer for about one hour or until slightly thickened. Chill. Pour over crepes and serve.

## Orange Seville

*Serves 16*

*This keeps nicely in the refrigerator for six to ten days. Serve with vanilla ice cream.*

¾ cup julienne of orange peel*
2 pounds fresh orange sections, about 10-12 oranges
2 cups sugar
1/8 teaspoon red food coloring
¼ cup brandy
¼ cup Grand Marnier

*Cut orange rind from washed navel oranges into thin julienne strips, 1/8 inch wide by 2½ inches long.

Combine orange julienne and two cups cold water in a saucepan, bring to a boil, and cook, covered, over moderate heat for 20 to 30 minutes. Remove from heat, drain, and cool the julienne in ice-cold water. Drain thoroughly and save the julienne for later use.

Peel away all white inner rind from oranges and separate into sections. Weigh for specified amount. Place the orange sections in a heavy saucepan. Add sugar and two cups cold water. Weight down orange sections with a plate or wire rack to prevent them from floating. Bring to a boil and simmer very gently for one hour. Remove the oranges from heat and let cool in the liquid.

With a slotted spoon, remove the oranges to a bowl. Combine the remaining liquid with the julienne, bring to a brisk boil, and continue cooking until reduced by half. Add red food coloring, stir to blend, and let cool.

Add brandy and Grand Marnier to the cool reduced liquid and stir well. Add orange sections and store, well-covered, in the refrigerator. Serve with ice cream.

## Black forest Cake

*Makes an 8-inch layer cake*

*Make or buy any good sponge cake to use when you concoct this unusual German cake with its cherry and butter cream filling.*

> 1 quart large black cherries, about 2 pounds
> ½ cup kirsch
> 1½ pounds confectioner's sugar (6¼ cups sifted)
> 3 tablespoons cornstarch
> 2 tablespoons cherry juice
> ½ pound butter
> 3 egg yolks
> 2 8-inch chocolate sponge cake layers, 1 inch thick
> 3 ounces bittersweet chocolate

Wash cherries and remove stems and seeds. Mix kirsch and one cup confectioner's sugar; pour over fruit in a saucepan. Let stand at least two hours; then heat to boiling. Mix cornstarch with about two tablespoons cherry juice and stir slowly into cherries. Boil and stir until slightly thickened, two to three minutes. Remove from heat and let cool. The consistency should be that of thin jelly.

Cream butter and remaining sugar until smooth. Beat in egg yolks and continue beating until mixture is light and fluffy.

Place one cake layer on plate. Make a half-inch border around edge with butter mixture and spread butter cream in a two-inch circle in center of cake. Spread cooled cherry mixture between the butter cream border and center. Place second cake layer on top, pressing down just enough to make layers stick together. Cover top and sides of both layers with remaining butter cream. Shave bittersweet chocolate over top.

## fROzen GRand maRnieR Souffle

*Serves 10 to 12*

*This is a superb light dessert with an exquisite flavor, and simple to prepare.*

- ¾ cup sugar
- 7 egg yolks
- 3 tablespoons Grand Marnier
- 2 tablespoons cognac
- ¼ cup frozen orange juice concentrate
- 2 cups heavy cream

Beat the sugar and egg yolks at high speed until light and fluffy. Add the Grand Marnier, cognac, and frozen orange juice concentrate at low speed.

In another bowl, whip the heavy cream at medium speed until soft, but not stiff.

Fold the two mixtures together until the whipped cream is completely incorporated.

Put into individual glasses (or a large souffle dish) with a three-inch band of wax paper around the edge, two inches extending above the top. Freeze overnight.

Remove wax paper and garnish with whipped cream and a cherry.

# Bananas nourries

*Serves 4*

*A dramatic flamed banana dessert, this is surprisingly simple to make.*

   8 tablespoons butter
   ¾ cup light brown sugar
   ½ cup banana liqueur
   4 bananas
   ¼ cup rum (151 proof)
   1 pint vanilla ice cream
   ½ cup roasted chopped hazelnuts

Slice bananas lengthwise

Heat butter in one large or two smaller skillets. Add brown sugar, and stir over medium to high heat until sugar dissolves and a caramel glaze is formed. Stir in banana liqueur. Lay bananas in the caramel glaze; cook, turning occasionally, for two minutes. Add rum and flame.

Serve each person two banana halves over two scoops of ice cream. Sprinkle with nuts.

# Menus

O NCE A MONTH AT THE ABBEY, we prepare an extraordinary feast for a limited number of people who attend our special "Gourmet Dinners." These dinners, usually presenting eight to ten courses with a separate wine to accompany each course, are a marvel of contrasts and culinary delights. Each of them might include an appetizer, a soup, a fish course, a salad, a game or fowl course, an intermezzo to cleanse the palate, the main meat course, dessert, and cheese, coffee, or liqueur.

As amazing as such a dinner might be, it is usually not practical to attempt entertaining on such a scale at home. We have attempted here, therefore, to suggest ways in which the recipes in this book might be combined to put together gourmet dinners that reflect the same principles as our monthly feasts at the Abbey. It will not be necessary at home, of course, to serve a different wine with each course; one may simply refer to the suggested wines listed after the recipe for each entree, and choose the wine that is within your price range.

To assemble menus on your own, only a few things need be kept in mind. If your first courses are heavy or elaborate, you will want to consider a lighter main course and dessert to set them off. Pay attention to the contrasts of temperature and taste among the various courses you present. Be watchful that at least some of the dishes can be prepared in part or in full well before the last minute; and take care not to allocate two dishes to the oven at the same time if they require different heats. Finally, do not neglect to notice the contrast of color and texture in the dishes that you array beside each other. It can be a disaster to serve trout, potatoes, and white asparagus spears together on the same plate, no matter how attractive the china or delectable the recipes!

---

Chilled Poached Salmon with Sauce Ravigote
Cream of Frog Leg Soup
Endives and Tomatoes with Neufchatel Dip
Roasted Tenderloin of Beef with Truffles and Pate de Fois Gras
Stuffed Artichoke Bottoms
White Asparagus with Brown Butter
Flamed Bananas Nourries

---

Avocado Stuffed with Crabmeat
Cream of Tomato Soup
Stuffed Breast of Chicken with Leeks and Watercress
Sauteed Cherry Tomatoes
Leaf Spinach
Saffron Rice
Crepes Fitzgerald

Duck Terrine with Pistachios
Lobster Bisque
Veal Cutlet filled with Mushrooms and Herbs
Zucchini stuffed with Tomatoes and Eggplant
Fresh Homemade Noodles
Black Forest Cake

---

Shrimp and Grapefruit Cocktail
Clear Oxtail Soup
Lamb Tenderloin with Veal Sweetbreads in Port Wine Sauce
Green Beans with Bacon
Potatoes Parisienne
Glazed Carrots
Strawberries Romanoff

---

Scallop Mousselines with Smoked Salmon
Fresh Spinach Salad with Duck Liver
Port Wine Sherbet
Roast Duckling with Green Peppercorns
Sauteed Snow Peas
Stuffed Mushroom Caps
Frozen Grand Marnier Souffle

---

Mushroom Caps filled with Louisiana Crabmeat "Dante"
Chilled Consomme with Caviar
Roast Quail with Grapes in Puff Pastry Nest
Champagne Sauerkraut with Pineapple
Baked Stuffed Tomatoes
Orange Seville

# Index

## A

Anchovy butter, 56
Appetizers
  artichoke with ragout and
    asparagus, 62–65
  avocado stuffed with crabmeat,
    66
  crabmeat mousseline, 70
  duck terrine with pistachios, 71–
    72
  endives and tomatoes with
    Neufchatel dip, 87
  king salmon with sweet mustard
    dill sauce, 73–74
  Louisiana crabmeat "Dante,"
    79–80
  Maine lobster, cold, with
    vegetable salad, 75–77
  mussels with spinach, 83–85
  poached salmon, chilled, 77–78
  Port wine sherbet, 86
  salmon mousseline, 70
  scallop mousselines with salmon,
    68–70
  shrimp and grapefruit cocktail,
    60–61
  snails in white wine herb sauce,
    81–82
  steak tartare with smoked eel,
    67–68
*Artichaut "Princesse" au Gratin,*
  62–65
Artichoke
  bottoms, stuffed, 185–86
  filled with fine ragout and
    asparagus, 62–65
Asparagus
  green, 171
  white, with brown butter, 170
*Asperges,* 170–71
Avocado stuffed with crabmeat, 66
*Avocat a l'Adam,* 66

## B

Bami Goreng, 100
Bananas Nourries, 202
Beans, green, with bacon, 176–77
Bearnaise sauce, 45–46
Beef
  filet, flamed with vodka, 137–38
  rib steak with red wine sauce and
    marrow, 146–47
  roast tenderloin of, with truffles
    and pate de foie gras, 139–40
  steak, strip loin, with mustard
    and green peppercorn sauce,
    141–42
  steak tartare with smoked eel,
    67–68
  stock, 4–5
  tenderloin strips in tomatoes and
    garlic, 142–43
  tournedos of tenderloin, 144–45
*Beurre Blanc,* 29
*Bisque de Homard,* 24–25
Black Forest cake, 200–201
*Boeuf Emince Nicoise,* 142–43
Bordelaise sauce, 30
*Bouillabaisse Marseillaise,* 98–99
Broccoli
  creamed, 181
  timbales, 182
*Broccolis a la Polonaise,* 171
*Brochette de Coquille St. Jacques
  aux Cepes,* 116–18
Brown stock, 5–6
Brussels sprouts, 172
Burgundy sauce, 36
Butter sauce, hot, 29
Butters
  anchovy, 56
  Colbert, 55
  fresh dill, 55
  lobster, 57
  maitre d'hotel, 55
  Montpellier, 58

# C

Cabbage, red, 173-74
*Cailles Roties a la Vigneronne,*
    127-28
*Canard Roti au Poivre Vert,* 128-
    29
*Canard Roti aux Fruits d'Or,* 130-
    31
*Carottes Glacees,* 175
Carrots, glazed, 175
*Cepes a la Provencale,* 179
Champagne sauerkraut, 174
    with pineapple, 174
*Champignons Farcis,* 177
*Chanterelles au Lardi,* 178
Chicken
    breast, with leek and watercress,
        132-34
    breast, in Port wine, 134-35
    lobster, and ham salad, 91-92
    mulligatawny, 19-20
    stock, 8
*Chou Rouge,* 173-74
*Choucroute au Vin de Champagne,*
    174-75
*Choux de Bruxelles,* 172
Colbert butter, 55
*Concombres a la Creme,* 184
*Concombres Farcis,* 184-85
Consomme, chilled, with caviar,
    13-14
*Consomme Double Froid a la
    Russe,* 13-14
*Cote de Boeuf a la Moelle
    Marchand de Vin,* 146-47
*Cotelettes d'Agneau Grille Maison,*
    156-57
*Courgettes Farcies,* 186-87
Crabmeat
    "Dante," 79-80
    mousselines, 70
    and vegetable salad, 88-89
Cream sauce, rich, 43
*Creme Fraiche,* 49
*Creme Milanaise,* 17-18

Crepes
    Fitzgerald, 198-99
    plain, 196-97
*Crevettes Cocktail Kempinski,* 60-
    61
Cucumber(s)
    in cream, 184
    salad with fresh dill, 95
    stuffed, 184-85

# D

Demi-glace, 6
Desserts
    bananas Nourries, 202
    Black Forest cake, 200-201
    crepes Fitzgerald, 198-99
    frozen Grand Marnier souffle,
        201
    orange Seville, 199-200
    strawberries Romanoff, 197
Dill butter, fresh, 55
Dover sole Regency, 111-13
Duck(ling)
    liver, with spinach salad, 89-90
    roast, with fresh fruit, 130-31
    roast, with green peppercorns,
        128-29
    terrine with pistachios, 71-72

# E

*Endives a la Neufchatel,* 87
Endives and tomatoes with
    Neufchatel dip, 87
*Entrecote au Poivre Vert,* 141-42
*Epinards a la Creme,* 181-82
*Epinards en Branches,* 180
*Escalope de Veau Nouvelle
    Bertram,* 148-50
*Escargots aux Fines Herbes,* 81-82

# F

*Faisan Roti Souvaroff,* 125-26
*Filet de Boeuf Flambe a la Russe,*
    137-38

Mushrooms
  stone, with tomatoes and garlic,
    179
  stuffed, 177
  wild, with bacon, 178
Mussels
  baked with spinach, 83–86
  with red snapper and tomato
    shrimp sauce, 106–8
  salad with saffron, 93–94
  soup of the Abbey, 20–22
Mustard dill sauce, sweet, 74
Mustard sauce, 37–38

Nasi Goreng, 100–101
New Orleans style seafood gumbo,
  22–23
*Noisettes d'Agneau au Porto,* 160–
  61
*Noisettes de Chevreuil Nouvelle
  Epoque,* 163–65
Noodles, fresh homemade, 192
*Nouilles Fraiches,* 192

O

*Oie Rotie a la Suedoise,* 123–24
*Oignons Glaces,* 175
Onions, pearl, glazed, 175
Orange sauce, 38–39
Orange Seville, 199–200
Oxtail soup
  clear, 11–12
  thickened clear, 13
  thickened unclarified, 13

P

Paprika cream sauce, 33–34
Pheasant, roast, in Madeira sauce,
  125–26
*Pommes de Terre Berny,* 191
*Pommes de Terre Parisienne,* 190
Pompano with shrimp, capers, and
  lemon, 118–19

Pork medallions Milanaise, 161–63
Port wine sherbet, 86
*Potage aux Grenouilles,* 16–17
Potato(es)
  Berny, 191
  and leek soup, chilled, 15
  Parisian, 190
Puff pastry, 195–96

Q

Quail, roast, with grapes and
  champagne kraut, 127–28
Quenelles, veal, 152–53

Rabbit, roast, in cream sauce, 166–
  67
Ratatouille, baked, 189–90
Ravigote sauce, 53
Red cabbage, 173–74
Red snapper with mussels and
  tomato shrimp sauce, 106–8
Rice, saffron, 193
*Risotto au Safran,* 193

S

*Salade a l'Abbe,* 91–92
*Salade Capri,* 164
*Salade de Concombres et Aneth,* 95
*Salade de Moules au Safran,* 93–94
*Salade des Epinards Nouvelle
  Epoque,* 89–90
*Salade Maison,* 88–89
Salads
  crabmeat and vegetable, 88–89
  cucumber, with dill, 95
  lobster, chicken, and ham, 91–92
  mussel, with saffron, 93–94
  spinach, with duck liver, 89–90
Salmon
  chilled, poached, with sauce
    Ravigote, 77–78
  marinated, with sweet mustard
    dill sauce, 73–74